PRAISE FOR *WINNING WELL: MAXIMI...*
COACH AND ATHLETE WELLNESS

CW00818949

"This is a great book for anyone just get
with years of experience. If you want to i
your team, as well as maximize the positiv ... you will have on your
athletes, this is a must have for your coaching library."—Jay Anderson, 2017
United Soccer Coaches National High School Coach of the Year and six-
time Montana Coaches Association Coach of the Year

"An absolute must read for all coaches and anyone who is in the business of
working with or managing people. *Winning Well* is a concise and articulate
roadmap to help coaches win at a higher level while also providing a better
people-centered process. All of my coaching friends will be getting a copy of
Winning Well in their stocking this Christmas!"—Matt Morris, MS CSCS,
head track and field/cross country coach, Colorado State University Pueblo

"As a former college athlete and Division I coach, I gained an appreciation
for what it takes to achieve success in sports both on and off the playing field.
Too often the approach to development can be very one dimensional. The
authors of *Winning Well* do a fantastic job of addressing the multifaceted role
of a coach and mentor and provide a detailed framework for success. It is well
worth the read!"—Pat Owen, three-time qualifier at the NCAA Wrestling
Championships, 2004 Big Ten Medal of Honor winner, and Harvard wrestling coach (2007–2012)

"Finding ways to make a difference is my biggest takeaway from what Cara
and Camille have put together here in *Winning Well*. The impact of coaching and the importance of fostering wellness is captured in this diverse range
of perspectives on what we do as coaches."—Cameron Kiosoglous, PhD,
assistant clinical professor and director of the Sport Coaching Leadership
Program at Drexel University, director of sports science for USRowing, and
education chair at the United States Center for Coaching Excellence

"As a coach and coach developer, I aim to center holistic athlete wellness and development. This book is a great resource for that: It provides much-needed, broad, and deep definitions for athlete-centered well-being. More than that, *Winning Well* includes practical tips and case studies to help coaches, coach developers, and athletes better understand how to care for themselves and one another. The language of inclusion, healing, and relationships permeates this book; those looking to unlock the power of sport will find *Winning Well* a wonderful tool to add to your toolkit of transformative coaching."
—**Julie McCleery, PhD, director of Research-Practice Partnerships, Center for Leadership in Athletics, University of Washington, and 25-plus years of coaching youth through elite sports**

"*Winning Well* provides great practical advice for supporting all athletes as they strive for excellence on and off the court. It's one of the first coaching books I've read that includes a much-needed formula for coaches in taking care of themselves as well. It's a desperately needed and refreshing take on inclusive coaching and doing the right thing for everyone in sports."
—**Kelly Graves, head coach of women's basketball at the University of Oregon, two-time Pac-12 Coach of the Year, and eight-time West Coast Conference Coach of the Year (Gonzaga University)**

"*Winning Well* is an invaluable resource for any coach looking to improve not only his or her winning record, but also the wellness of individual athletes, the coaching staff, and the program as a whole. This book approaches coaching from a place of inclusion and respect, and is aimed at making athletes feel safe and supported in their athletic programs. It provides coaches with information on how to model healthy interactions and address every facet of wellness to produce winning programs, successful athletes, and better humans."
—**Jamie Schlueter, MD, team physician at the University of Portland, for USA Women's Ice Hockey, and for USA Paralympic Track and Field**

Winning Well

PROFESSIONAL DEVELOPMENT IN SPORT COACHING

Published in partnership with the United States Center for Coaching Excellence

Series Editor: Karen Collins

This book series provides coaches, sport organization leaders, directors of coaching, educators, and athletic directors with the skills, guidelines, and research-based best practices to support quality coach development. Offering practical, readily implemented information, these books will help to improve coaching performance across multiple sport contexts.

To Be a Better Coach: A Guide for the Youth Sport Coach and Coach Developer by Pete Van Mullem and Lori Gano-Overway

Winning Well: Maximizing Coach and Athlete Wellness by Cara Cocchiarella and Camille Adana

Winning Well

Maximizing Coach and Athlete Wellness

CARA COCCHIARELLA
CAMILLE ADANA

ROWMAN & LITTLEFIELD
Lanham • Boulder • New York • London

Published by Rowman & Littlefield
An imprint of The Rowman & Littlefield Publishing Group, Inc.
4501 Forbes Boulevard, Suite 200, Lanham, Maryland 20706
www.rowman.com

6 Tinworth Street, London, SE11 5AL, United Kingdom

British Library Cataloguing in Publication Information Available

Library of Congress Cataloging-in-Publication Data

Names: Cocchiarella, Cara, 1979– author. | Adana, Camille, 1976– author.
Title: Winning well : maximizing coach and athlete wellness / Cara Cocchiarella, Camille Adana.
Description: Lanham, Maryland : Rowman & Littlefield, [2021] | Series: Professional Development in Sport Coaching / series editor: Karen Collins | "Published in partnership with the United States Center for Coaching Excellence"—T.p. recto. | Includes bibliographical references and index. | Summary: "Using the eight dimensions of wellness—physical, social, emotional, intellectual, spiritual, environmental, occupational, and financial—this book encourages coaches to invest in their own wellness alongside that of their athletes to make a lasting impact and propel their athletes toward excellence"—Provided by publisher.
Identifiers: LCCN 2021017383 (print) | LCCN 2021017384 (ebook) | ISBN 9781538157930 (Paperback : acid-free paper) | ISBN 9781538157947 (ePub)
Subjects: LCSH: Coaches (Athletics)—Training of. | Coaching (Athletics) | Physical fitness.
Classification: LCC GV711 .C65 2021 (print) | LCC GV711 (ebook) | DDC 796.07/7—dc23
LC record available at https://lccn.loc.gov/2021017383
LC ebook record available at https://lccn.loc.gov/2021017384

Contents

Acknowledgments

Our lives have been transformed by coaches who guided our pursuit of excellence both on and off the field of play. They supported our wellness by investing in us as people and inspired us to continue to learn from every athlete and coach who has crossed our paths. In *Winning Well*, we aim to foster the gift of that opportunity to make a lasting, positive impact through inclusive, holistic coaching and coach development. We are humbled to contribute to coach and athlete wellness alongside our colleagues in the field.

We want to thank our family and friends who believed in us and supported our passion. Significant gratitude goes out to the coaches and athletes who contributed stories, statements, and perspectives. The patience, time, and insight provided by Erika Martin, Melissa Mulick, Tamika Herbert, and others made a substantial impact. We thank the United States Center for Coaching Excellence and Rowman & Littlefield for their collaboration and role in helping us bring this vision to life.

Introduction

What did your coaches teach you? How have their efforts impacted your life?

While sports experiences vary from being incredibly positive to detrimental or even traumatic, the influence of athletics goes beyond just a game played by a set of arbitrary rules. Within the bounds of the challenges accepted by athletes are many key participants: other competitors, officials, teammates, and—possibly most integral to the experience—coaches.[1]

Asked to identify the most meaningful or impactful lessons taught by coaches, it is unlikely that many people would respond with a specific strategy, tactical concept, or physical skill. Of course, those are all essential components of a sport that someone may learn from a coach, but what really sticks tends to go far beyond the boundaries of the field of play. Responses from an Olympic athlete may or may not differ considerably from that of a multisport high school star, recreational adult competitor, or youth league participant. What is likely to be most consistent is that the lessons imparted by coaches upon athletes are bigger than just the game itself.

Although sports provide the vehicle for learning that has the potential to permanently alter a person's way of living, for better or worse, those lessons are transferable to life outside of athletics.[2] Such efforts by coaches are classified as powerful, inspiring, and life changing. One need not go much further than the two questions at the top of this page to find a range of answers encompassing all aspects of a person's well-being. Coaches who take stock in the holistic wellness of the athletes they coach are positioned to ensure their lessons are capacity-building, inclusive, and empowering.[3]

It does not take a world-renowned coaching career to make a lasting difference for athletes. As leaders in sports, coaches have the opportunity to guide athletes to championships of all varieties, lay the foundation for perseverance, build confidence, and forge lasting connections with others—to name a few. Opportunities such as these start at the individual level and permeate into society. When humans become the focal point of our work in sports, we hold the power to change the world; applying the concepts of wellness allows us to do so in a manner that is inclusive and deeply fulfilling. Like any source of power, with the potential impact of sports comes daunting responsibility. It is on all of us who lead within the world of athletics to ensure that power is being used for good—that as we strive to win, we are always focused on winning well.

WHO THIS BOOK IS FOR

Winning Well is for coaches who value, or would like to value, the humans involved in sports. It's for coaches who want to improve their coaching practice, particularly those who want to improve their own lives and maximize the positive impact they have on athletes. It's for coaches who think about and employ wellness-enhancing strategies consistently, occasionally, or never. Where this model is universal in nature is that it has been created for coaches who want to win *and* make a difference.

Using a wellness framework allows us to improve the world of athletics for everyone involved—from the coach developer to the athlete. This book is for paid and unpaid coaches in all settings (schools, clubs, community leagues, etc.) who work with athletes ranging in age from elementary school through college. It is for coaches in their first year and coaches in their one hundred and first year. If you want to invest in players as people, help them to build skills for success in life outside of sports, and maximize their health and well-being, both on and off the court, *while* winning competitions, this is the book for you.

WHAT THIS BOOK ISN'T

This isn't a book that you will just breeze through aimlessly. It is intended to inspire your engagement. It isn't focused solely on the fun and easy side of coaching. Uncomfortable realities are revealed and moving stories are shared because true growth requires awareness, authenticity, and passion. *Winning*

Well isn't a fix-all prescription that tells you exactly what to do, at every moment, with your sports program.

WHAT THIS BOOK IS

Simply put, *Winning Well* is about bringing humanity back into coaching and sports. It is no secret that in all industries, even the most intense, caring about and investing in the humans who make up the system is necessary to realize long-term success.[4] We simply cannot forget that there are *people* involved in athletics. According to Bo Hanson, "Most of all, coaches must understand that they are in the people industry. Sport is played by people, coached by people, and managed by people; if coaches do not understand how to work incredibly well with people who are similar to and different from themselves, they are destined to fail."[5] This book is a manual for getting started in the process of investing in wellness, changing practices that don't support people holistically, and/or building upon the great work you are already doing with others in your sport and the world.

When it comes to coaching people, we have a tendency to ignore our most basic needs. We must always attend to wellness essentials before we can expect learning, growth, or development to occur. You may hear this concept described as "Maslow before Bloom."[6] We cannot expect growth to occur in athletes if they are hungry, tired, or feeling unsafe or insecure. We must ensure their needs (Maslow's Hierarchy of Needs) are met before we can delve into the best means for teaching them (Bloom's Taxonomy of Learning).

We've all heard and read too many stories of coaches and athletes being neglected as people in the name of competition. It's not okay. There is no dichotomy here. Whoever told us that we can either support wellness *or* support championship performances was wrong. Not only can we do both simultaneously, but it is our *duty* to do so.

This book presents a practical, much needed model to the world of coaching. Theories on leadership and coaching, current research, and personal testimonies supporting the framework will be provided. A selected bibliography of additional coach development resources that establish a foundation for wellness-enhancing coaching efforts is included.

The concept of *Winning Well* is not intended to be taken as a prescriptive step-by-step process. You are provided with many principles to consider, questions to ponder, and ideas to try, depending upon the context in which you coach. The goal is for you to choose what you need, what fits your coaching philosophy and personality, what makes sense in your program at this time, and what is most applicable to the athletes with whom you work. That can change from day to day or even moment to moment, so allow this to serve as a handbook used throughout time. In employing this model, there will always be room for growth.

Sports have the potential to make a lasting impact on the lives of all participants in part because of their competitive nature. Most of us want to win as often as possible, and because of the intensity of the effort we put into our sport, the lessons we learn are more meaningful and applicable than those we learn elsewhere. Taking advantage of the environment to teach what truly matters not only changes lives but also translates to wins on the field. With that spirit in mind, it is a coach's responsibility to help athletes realize success—defined in as many ways as possible.

WHY YOUR PERSONAL WELLNESS MATTERS IN ADDITION TO ATHLETE WELLNESS

Example is not the main thing in influencing others. It is the only thing.

—*Albert Schweitzer*

Wellness is an essential component of effective coaching.[7] In the intense world of sports, as teams, athletes, and coaches strive for excellence in performance, the importance of wellness is heightened. While this book will focus on helping you to coach and guide athletes to their best, your own personal wellness will play an essential role in this venture. Not only will players emulate your wellness practices or lack thereof, but if you are struggling on a personal level, you will certainly not bring your best to your coaching.

Asking hard questions and self-reflecting is an essential step in this process. According to Hanson, "Self-awareness is the cornerstone of personal effectiveness in any leadership role."[8] Much like we need to ensure athletes are always treated as whole people, coaches should do the same for themselves.[9]

Role modeling is one of the most permanent, effective, and broadly applied teaching methods at our disposal. Because of the efficiency of role modeling and how easily it can be used in all of our teachings, we teach all the time subconsciously—we teach who we are.[10]

Who you are is an absolutely essential consideration in your coaching.[11] Coaches' behaviors and attitudes will be replicated by players on a regular basis. As we have seen across the board in athletics, this is either amazingly productive or frighteningly detrimental. For athletes and coaches, there is no hiding—sports reveal character and identity. Consequently, coaches must consistently demonstrate integrity—doing the right thing when they think no one is watching.

MAKING INCLUSION THE FOUNDATION OF ALL OUR WORK

Culturally inclusive practices have always been important, and yet we have an *incredibly* long way to go. Consistent critical examination and recognition of one's own judgments and stereotypes are essential in terms of personal growth and progress in society. We all bring our identities, experiences, and biases with us everywhere we go. Constantly working to expand our understanding of ourselves, others, and how we all interact is key. If we don't develop authentic relationships with others whose lived experiences are different from our own, we are limited to only our own personal realities and what society and media have taught us about others. How you feel and what you do in this regard will undoubtedly impact your professional work.

Empathy is a central theme of this book. Being empathetic means not simply understanding another's experience but embracing the fact that others have valuable stories unique to their lives that deserve our attention, trust, and compassion.[12] Empathy requires wholeheartedly accepting the fact that barriers exist, people have been wronged, and disenfranchising, discriminating systems are in place throughout every sector of society. Each of us fits somewhere in those systems; we don't get to just stand outside of it all. We owe it to one another to take the necessary steps to build maximal empathy for others within ourselves.

In relation to wellness specifically, it is important to note that there are a multitude of barriers one may experience in an effort to reach their greatest potential. Whether related to race, color, gender, socioeconomic status, religion, sexual orientation, ability level, or any other factor, the sports experience and maintaining wellness may look very different for each person. It is our duty to seek out and minimize barriers to wellness for all while promoting equity and accessibility.

This book uses gender-neutral language and employs culturally inclusive thought processes and efforts, *and undoubtedly, there are still mistakes*. It is our job—all of us—to look into different dimensions of identity and determine how to best create inclusive spaces. It takes intentional action to recognize who we are in a space and to see others in that same space *as they are*. It may be challenging, especially at first, but inclusion is critical, powerful, and worth the effort—every time.

WELLNESS IN COACH DEVELOPMENT

Coach development and coach education are complementary yet unique components of a comprehensive professional growth plan, and they play an essential role in advancing the coaching profession. While coach education encompasses formalized processes (certification programs, etc.), coach development is viewed as the combination of informal learning experiences that advance coaching (attending workshops, working with a mentor, practicing and reflecting, etc.).[1] Coach education plays a vital role in developing common language, expectations, and practices to promote healthy sports participation. By nature, coach development plans and efforts are influential due to the potential to tailor informal learning to meet the specific needs of any given coach within the context of their coaching role. This book will focus on coach development and assisting coach developers in applying the material on an individual basis with coaches.

How coach development looks for any one coach may be unique; however, the key components of the process remain the same. Using a coaching framework to determine the essential skills and competencies a coach should develop within their context (sport, age of athletes, competitive level, etc.), coach developers are able to build effective, differentiated learning plans for each individual with whom they work.[2] Ensuring that efforts are centered on not only "what to coach" but also "how to coach," coach developers are positioned to help coaches maximize their efficiency and effectiveness in a manner that suits each coach individually.

Helping to promote the educational roots of the coaching profession is integral.[3] Coach developers are positioned for substantial impact when they are able to advance coaches' skills in teaching. It is important to keep in mind the shift in perspective that you may be promoting for the coaches with whom you work. Because coach education is often mandated and has traditionally placed an emphasis on the technical and tactical aspects of sport, coach development efforts will demand open-mindedness and buy-in on the part of the coach. How you connect with coaches in this regard may impact both the effectiveness of your work along with the human experience of coaching, which is something we must all continue to value. A strong developmental plan for coaches is well supplemented with the material in this book, while the wellness framework provides structure for holistically supporting coaches as people.

For the coach developer, this book serves as a resource to help you reinforce the value and need for wellness in sports for both coaches and athletes. A thorough understanding of the eight dimensions of wellness provides you with a structure for identifying and addressing wellness issues with coaches. The rationale for emphasizing each of the dimensions may bring to light areas for improvement within programs that you support. The tips and barriers that are included are not all-inclusive and you will almost certainly have more to add. Athletes' and coaches' stories are included as a powerful vehicle for sharing the impact of wellness-enhancing efforts and are meant to be passed along to help inspire others to invest in coach and athlete wellness. Wellness is a relatively neglected aspect of coaching and sports, and your investment in this work is essential in helping to promote coaching that is more holistic and inclusive. Advocating for wellness through coach development efforts supports happier, healthier, more fulfilled coaches and their capacity to lead athletes to excellence on and off the field of play.

Notes

1. Sarah McQuade, "Current Models of Coach Education, Training, and Certification," in *Coach Education Essentials: Your Guide to Developing Sport Coaches*, edited by Kristen Dieffenbach and Melissa Thompson (Champaign, IL: Human Kinetics, 2020), 187–208.

2. McQuade, "Current Models of Coach Education, Training, and Certification"; Penny Crisfield, "Long-Term Coach Development Process," in *Coach Education Essentials: Your Guide to Developing Sport Coaches*, edited by Kristen Dieffenbach and Melissa Thompson (Champaign, IL: Human Kinetics, 2020), 281–308.

3. Crisfield, "Long-Term Coach Development Process"; Kristen Dieffenbach, "Frameworks for Coach Education and Development," in *Coach Education Essentials: Your Guide to Developing Sport Coaches*, edited by Kristen Dieffenbach and Melissa Thompson (Champaign, IL: Human Kinetics, 2020), 3–16.

WELLNESS

You don't win with Xs and Os. What you win with is people.

—*Joe Gibbs*

There are literally millions of routes to take in working effectively with others and this book provides one that is universal and ever expanding. Wellness is innately human. It is multidimensional, constantly changing, and it has no end. Its qualities and characteristics formulate an ideal launching point for a coaching book focused on the people in sports.

What Is Wellness?

According to the National Wellness Institute, wellness is defined as "an active process through which people become aware then make choices toward a more successful existence."[13] The institute goes on to highlight the importance of those choices, stating, "Mindfully focusing on wellness in our lives builds resilience and enables us to thrive amidst life's challenges." This sets the stage for what is communicated and advanced in this book. For everyone involved, that means crushing it on and off the field of play.

In this book, eight dimensions of wellness will be addressed that are all interrelated. One aspect can (and likely will) impact any or all of the others. Interactions between dimensions can be simple and obvious or they can be difficult to identify; such interactions are countless. If we embrace their existence, we can use this knowledge to our advantage. A challenging interaction between dimensions of wellness is demonstrated by getting "hangry": a physical need for food may lead to emotional distress. A helpful connection between dimensions may be experienced when someone learns. Developing an intellectual understanding of themselves may shift their values, adjusting their spiritual wellness.

To thrive in terms of wellness, it is essential to value all aspects of wellness. We can compensate with one aspect where we may be weak in others, but to be our best, we must emphasize all of the dimensions to some extent, simultaneously.[14]

The dimensions of wellness addressed in each chapter of this book include physical, social, emotional, intellectual, spiritual, environmental, occupational, and financial.[15] Each dimension will be defined in terms of how it specifically fits into the world of sports, and a rationale concerning its role in building champion performers and champions for life will be provided. Each section will address current problems and inequities. You will be guided through a short reflection of your current understandings, priorities, and practices in relation to each dimension. Tips will be provided for you to use at your discretion for building each particular type of wellness in yourself and in athletes. Finally, stories from the field are shared to demonstrate wellness at work, incorporating numerous voices to provide valuable, diverse perspectives. In appendixes B through D, you'll find assessments you can use to measure your current wellness, as well as your support for athlete wellness.

The Wellness Wheel

It is common to see multidimensional wellness models depicted in a wheel format. Because the dimensions are interrelated, the image and concept of a wheel is an apt representation and lends itself naturally to self-assessments. To use the wellness wheel as an awareness building tool, complete the following steps:

1. Assess each dimension of wellness on a scale of 0 to 10, based on how you feel things are going in that aspect of your life. A score of 0 represents a lack of wellness in that dimension of your life and a score of 10 indicates complete fulfillment.
2. Plot the score associated with your current assessment on the line that corresponds to each dimension, and then connect those scores, moving around the wheel from one dimension to the next.
3. Reflect on your scores and the shape of your wheel as it relates to your current behaviors.

The resulting shape provides a visual to help you recognize the influence of each dimension on the others and on your wellness as a whole. Participants are encouraged to think about the ability of the wheel to roll (although it is important to also strive for a large wheel as opposed to a tiny round wheel that might roll perfectly). Figures 0.1 and 0.2 demonstrate how a blank and completed wellness wheel might look.

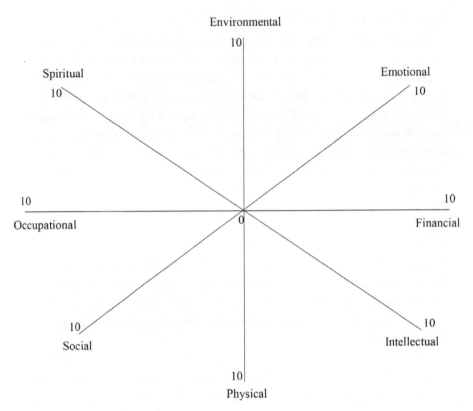

FIGURE 0.1
Blank Wellness Wheel

The wellness wheel can be an incredibly powerful tool. It opens our eyes to aspects of our lives that we may not normally ponder. It highlights our priorities and can also give us some insight to our current strengths and weaknesses. The assessment is context specific, however, so what is happening in the world around us may have a big impact on the results. Finally, it is important to recognize that "perfection"—a perfectly round wheel with all 10s—is likely impossible. There is no reason for anyone to beat themselves up about a less than perfect wheel. There will always be room for growth with this model.

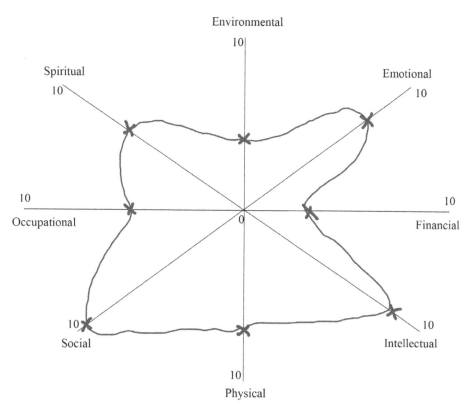

FIGURE 0.2
Completed Wellness Wheel

Completing the wellness wheel *now* allows you to examine your personal wellness and your support for athlete wellness, as a preassessment (which is an integral step in self-improvement). As you develop a deeper understanding of the dimensions of wellness and how they apply, you will want to revisit this activity. Consider also evaluating athletes' wellness or having them evaluate their own, in a safe environment and an age-appropriate manner. Completing the wheel from time to time allows you to make comparisons and evaluate the efficiency of your current efforts.

APPLICATIONS IN COACH DEVELOPMENT: USING THE WELLNESS WHEEL

As a coach developer, you are encouraged to use the wellness wheel (along with the assessments by dimension in appendixes B through D) with the coaches with whom you work. Typically, wellness wheels are conducted as self-assessments that provide a foundation for further conversation and learning, but outside perspectives may also be of value. You yourself can assess a coach's personal wellness or their support for athlete wellness. You may also want to consider suggesting additional outside feedback, such as that provided by athletes. Athletes' opinions about how well a coach supports their wellness within each dimension may be particularly meaningful and serve as a guide for potential focal points in coach development.

Wellness is a personal endeavor, and you will need coaches' sincere engagement to help them enhance their wellness. The results of the wellness wheel assessment may reveal clear areas for improvement, or they may simply help you to get to know the coach better. As you build trust with coaches, using this tool allows you to connect with them personally and demonstrate your concern for their well-being. Keep in mind this may feel very vulnerable for coaches. You will need to ensure that they feel safe with you to use the wellness wheel authentically. Safety and trust are essential components of a productive coach–coach developer relationship and play an integral role in helping you both to complete your work.[1]

Note

1. François Rodrigue and Pierre Trudel, "A 'Personal Learning Coach' for High-Performance Coaches," in *Coach Education and Development in Sport: Instructional Strategies*, edited by Bettina Callary and Brian Gearity (New York: Routledge, 2020), 141–53.

Physical Wellness

As an athlete, you only have so much time. The window only has so much time and then it closes. You have to take care of yourself the best you can.

—*Barry Bonds*

WHAT IS PHYSICAL WELLNESS IN THE CONTEXT OF SPORTS?
Physical wellness involves all the efforts we put forth to achieve and maintain optimal health. It builds a base that we (quite literally) cannot live without. We all have physical limits, and within those limits we can strive to reach our personal potential. Physical wellness, especially for athletes, must include eating well, coping with stress, getting adequate sleep, and feeling confident in their bodies. Even the best workouts and exercise physiology concepts are effective only when applied through a holistic physical wellness lens.

WHY DOES PHYSICAL WELLNESS MATTER IN THE WORLD OF ATHLETICS?
There is an increased level of complexity to physical wellness when competition is involved. This is true for both coaches and athletes. Whether you are trying to crush an opponent or are looking to surpass goals on a personal level, you are going beyond just hoping that you can easily maneuver a flight of stairs. If the goal is optimal performance, you must invest in efforts to support your best physical self.

Prioritizing physical wellness is something that coaches and athletes ideally internalize for a lifetime. It sets the foundation for lifelong love for sports, movement, and fitness. Finding the balance between training and staying healthy is key. All other factors being equal, a physically healthy athlete will outperform an unhealthy athlete every time (keeping in mind that undertraining an athlete is a safer bet than overtraining, which may lead to numerous health issues). Much is known about the human body and how to make it perform at the top of its game, and all bodies respond a little differently. As a coach, you should employ those concepts that are most applicable to the level of the athletes you coach, gaining awareness of what works best for each individual. There is no doubt that a well-trained athlete has a better chance of winning than one who is not.

Physical wellness can also be viewed as the promotion of athlete safety. The combination of the actions you take to keep athletes safe should be of paramount importance. Safety trainings, minimizing risks in the environment, and using additional resources available to you all contribute to building a safe space. Within your safety plan, it is also essential to attend to individual athletes' needs (injuries, allergies, etc.). Coaches who are focused on safety are aware of and constantly surveying the facilities and equipment for potential risks or hazards. Before you get into any of the technical aspects of your sport, you must ensure that your athletes are protected from harm to the best of your ability.

PROBLEM: WE AREN'T TAKING CARE OF THE BODIES THAT ARE OUT THERE TRYING TO PERFORM AT THEIR PEAK!

A variety of issues prevent athletes from realizing their physical potential. Leaders in athletics face the following challenges, among others: societal inequities, a sports culture that neglects wellness, misinformation in the food and fitness industries, and abusive coaching practices.

First, and important to note, are some of the extreme discrepancies between individuals' lives. Factors that impede physical wellness for athletes may include food and housing insecurity, lack of emotional and physical safety at home, and stressful environments that interrupt the potential to rest and sleep as needed. On the flip side, we also see players being overworked physically and falling victim to unrealistic expectations imposed by media, the culture of a specific sport, and coaching practices. Physical wellness is important, especially when there is a high-performance goal involved, but there has to be a balance.

The world of athletics is riddled with dilemmas that have been documented and are thankfully being addressed by experts across the domain. The Aspen Institute provides pertinent research, scholarly recommendations, and practical tips associated with the current troubles we face in sports.[1] The system we have built is seeing a dramatic decline in participation, especially among low-income populations and athletes of color. Some of the factors that contribute to this sad state include early sports specialization, year-round participation, pay-to-play models, overuse injuries, and burnout.

Due to the amount of money available in the fitness and nutrition industries, there is an abundance of misleading information that coaches may pass on to athletes (directly or indirectly). Sifting through the sources to determine which ones are reliable and which ones are ineffective or may lead to harm is a challenge. As a coach, it is your responsibility to educate yourself about the topics in which you need additional insight and find appropriate resources to reference and share.

When we do our part in helping athletes to fuel their bodies for success, we must also address the disordered eating tendencies that plague sports culture. Promoting fueling for performance through a body-positive lens is something that sports culture has failed to do in the past.[2] Regardless of the sport you coach and the gender, age, or competitive level of your athletes, this is a topic that should not be avoided. With younger players, you may not get into the specifics about different sources of protein, but conversations about fueling for play are still valuable.[3]

This is the unfortunate truth: Some specific coaching practices and competitive strategies are apparently living in the past. There are still coaches out there who blatantly disregard athletes' wellness. We hear stories about athletes like Mary Cain, who was driven to disordered eating and resulting physical, psychological, and emotional ailments due to outdated coaching practices.[4] As a long-distance runner, her weight was regularly displayed to teammates and she was chastised for even the slightest gains. Like all athletes, Cain was also exposed to standard cultural expectations that may promote body shaming and dysmorphia. While there may be an ideal body weight or size for competing, athletes are not just robots waiting for their next calculated physical adjustment.

Sacrificing the physical wellness of an athlete in the name of gaining a competitive advantage is wrong. We have seen this in virtually all sports, in a variety of shapes and forms. Sometimes it is overworking athletes. Sometimes it is ignoring injuries and pushing through safety procedures. Sometimes it is over-the-top nutritional expectations and caloric restriction or forced over-eating. We are informed enough to know better. It doesn't work in relation to helping athletes reach their physical potential or optimize performance, and it definitely doesn't work in light of their overall wellness. While we tend to see increased prevalence of such issues in certain sports, *every* athlete is trying to figure all of this out to some degree. Like other inclusive practices, the efforts we make to support those who are most impacted also help to support the health and wellness of all.

Through the lens of physical wellness, coaches can help to reverse the aforementioned tragic trends. If we truly focus on the wellness of the people involved, we can build the structures to support optimizing physical wellness, minimizing injury, and maintaining a thriving sports community.

A NOTE ON FEASIBILITY AS IT RELATES TO PHYSICAL WELLNESS

Before discussing practical tips and ideas, we need to reflect on the realities of athletes' lives. Very rarely is promoting wellness as simple as it seems, and it is essential that we all approach the process with empathy and compassion. In relation to maximizing physical wellness, a few barriers that you may encounter include, but are not limited to, the following:

- Everyone has physical limits, and how these look for each athlete will vary.
- Eating a balanced diet requires not only education about nutrition but also financial access.
- Physical safety is a fundamental human need. Consider your athletes' environment and how safe or unsafe they may feel on a regular basis. Not meeting this need may manifest itself in a variety of ways.
- There is a wide range of intensities and different sources of stress that may be experienced by athletes.
- The processes of rest, recovery, and sleep may be extremely impacted in the lives of some athletes, leading to physical, mental, and/or emotional consequences.

- Access to equipment and facilities may influence athletes' fitness levels and/ or sport-specific opportunities. Some athletes will naturally be more raw than others based on the resources available to them, and as a result, their physical needs will vary.

While this list is not exhaustive, taking the time to acknowledge potential barriers to wellness is imperative. Coaches and athletes alike have quite a bit to consider when it comes to maximizing their wellness potential.

Physical wellness in sports supports fueling for performance, appropriate physical training, stress management, adequate sleep, rest, and recovery, as is feasible, and fosters a love for physical activity and play.

WHERE ARE YOU NOW?

I think self-awareness is probably the most important thing towards becoming a champion.

—*Billie Jean King*

The following questions pertaining to each dimension of wellness that are presented in this section will help guide you through general reflection throughout the book. More pointed questions for each dimension can be found in the Wellness Assessments by Dimension (appendixes B through D).

Be honest in your reflection; there are no right or wrong answers. This is intended to help build awareness of your current knowledge, beliefs, and behaviors.

1. How do you feel about your current physical wellness?
2. How do you feel about the physical wellness of the athletes you coach?
3. How much of a priority is it for you to support your athletes' physical wellness?
4. How well-informed and prepared do you feel to help maximize physical wellness in the athletes you coach?

5. How do your personal and coaching practices support or detract from your athletes' physical wellness?

TIPS FOR SUPPORTING YOUR OWN PHYSICAL WELLNESS

Coaching doesn't make you immune to the risks associated with neglecting physical health. The following are some tips to help avoid such issues:

- At all points in the season your body needs movement. Whether it is a short walk or an intense workout, the benefits of movement are irrefutable, especially during times of stress.
- When possible, consider completing pre- or postseason workouts, participating in drills in some way, or play with the team. Players will appreciate seeing you active, especially as you work to push them to be their best.
- If feasible, participate in workout classes of your own. This can serve as a reminder of how it feels to push yourself and what it's like to be coached.
- Listen to your body. When you feel like you need to wiggle, run around, pump some iron, or stretch—do it.
- Fueling your body for success is necessary even if you aren't physically competing yourself. All human bodies manage different nutrients in unique ways. Pay attention to your physical responses to food and how you feel when you eat and/or avoid specific foods.
- Water is essential. Aim to consume half of your body weight (in pounds) in ounces each day.
- Eat your veggies and fruits! Prioritize variety and fill your plate with a lot of colorful produce. Maximize fresh, local, and seasonal options to the best of your ability, but don't let that be a barrier to healthy eating.
- Focus on lean meats that are grass-fed and naturally raised, if feasible, or other healthy protein sources.
- Consume complex carbohydrates over simple carbs. Especially in periods of intense activity, the body likes to use carbohydrates as a fuel source. Choose carbohydrates that provide your body with fiber and that won't spike your blood sugars.
- Minimize alcohol consumption. Beyond the horrible physical experience of a hangover, alcohol is a depressant that affects our sleep, mood, and productivity.

- Immune-boosting and disease-fighting foods (such as foods high in anti-oxidants) are critical to prevent you from getting sick.
- When it comes to evaluating the credibility of nutrition information, apply common sense. If something feels like a quick fix and/or unrealistic, it probably is.
- Take your time with meals, eat with others, and minimize distractions. Experts suggest that a focus on how and why we eat is equally important to what we eat.[5] Enjoy your food as opposed to inhaling it at max speed.
- Identify times of stress and give your body what it needs to persevere. It is easy to let stress take over, stop physical activity, fuel our bodies carelessly, and lie in bed awake at night. This vicious cycle has the potential to destroy our physical wellness. Putting our bodies into the fight, flight, or freeze response consistently over time can be harmful.
- Maintaining a reasonable sleep schedule helps to regulate sleep and can improve the quality of sleep dramatically. Guidelines for all adults encourage a minimum of eight hours.[6] It can be very tempting to stay up late, mulling over coaching decisions and putting together game and practice plans; however, that is problematic. Coaches can save significant time by employing more efficient coaching practices to work smarter, not harder.
- Minimize late-night distractions and electronics. Staying up all hours of the night watching film doesn't actually make players better out on the field. Athletes need concerted practice and coaches need their sleep.
- Avoid caffeine later in the day, and don't get sucked into thinking that the mental stimulation you feel from a cup of coffee is the same thing as being rested. Like energy drinks, coffee doesn't supply any sort of physical energy. It just provides a temporary, artificial boost in brain activity—and often perpetuates detrimental habits.

TIPS FOR SUPPORTING ATHLETES' PHYSICAL WELLNESS

One of your primary roles is to show athletes—through your actions—how to maintain physical wellness. You should have direct conversations about the four primary concerns discussed earlier: physical activity, fueling your body, coping with stress, and sleep. Not communicating about these sensitive topics sends a strong message in itself and promotes a harmful system.[7] Construct practice and workout plans that push players to improve, but do not go beyond healthy limits. Look for signals that things either are working for athletes or need to be adjusted, and consider the following tips for supporting physical wellness in athletes:

- Look into all the risks to which athletes may be exposed and ensure you have a plan to keep them safe.[8] Complete required safety trainings, ensure your staff has done the same, and consistently look for potential hazards to eliminate or minimize. In addition, educate yourself about sport-specific dangers and all individual health issues on your team.
- Work to inspire a love of sports and fitness to promote activity for life.
- Find a balance between deliberate practice and deliberate play that is appropriate for the developmental and competitive levels of the athletes.[9] Skills are important, but so are enjoyment and motivation, especially if we want to build athletes' investment in the game. They can play by previously established rules and safety guidelines. It doesn't have to be a free-for-all, but they don't need you in the way all the time (unless you want to join as a participant).[10] For example, you might allow players to warm up with ten minutes of free play before your structured practice begins.
- Use the training resources available to you. Long-term athlete development (LTAD) models serve as an excellent starting point for delving into well-formulated physical training plans.[11] The national governing bodies of your sport may even provide sport-specific athlete development plans.
- Keep in mind, physical training is multifaceted. It should be specific to athletes' goals and based on principles of training:[12]
  - Progression: Technical skills and physical capacity must be built gradually to move toward a more advanced state.
  - Overload: An increase in the frequency, intensity, and/or time of workouts is required for physical adaptation to occur.
  - Individuality: Everyone is different and responds differently to workouts.
  - Specificity: Improving any skill requires practicing that specific skill.
  - Recovery: The body must rest to repair itself and allow for physical adaptation.
  - Reversibility: Physical adaptations are lost when training is stopped.
- Construct workouts and practice plans that challenge athletes to be their best with realistic limits. Encourage players' maximal efforts and *stop* when there is anything of concern. Take cues from what they are telling

you directly—and what they are not. Athletes will start to recognize what works best for them as well as their bodies' impressive potential. They will discover the physical feelings associated with growth and improvement and will start to learn how to listen to their own bodies.

- Explicitly teach athletes the value and importance of rest and recovery for health and performance. The goal is twofold: to prevent overtraining and to allow the physiological benefits of hard work to take hold. Much of that recovery takes place when they are sleeping.
- Encourage athletes to be honest about injuries. To help players stay in the game as much as possible, we need to be informed about injuries so that we can help them determine the best plan for their long-term health and recovery.
- Unless you are a sports medicine doctor, build a connection with one and seek their advice on player injuries.
- Be informed about concussion protocols and follow them exactly as intended. No practice, play, or game will ever be more important than a player's life, and that risk is real when it comes to head injuries.
- Build a culture that emphasizes player safety and encourages athletes to be transparent about their own and teammates' injuries. Playing through discomfort is one thing, but neglecting the advice of medical professionals and/or playing through *pain* is another.
- Sports nutrition may be a key topic that you want to address at length, and if you don't have a background in nutrition yourself, bring on the experts! There is no shame in reaching out. Ensure that the person who will talk to your athletes will do so through a body-positive, fueling-for-performance lens, and then take in as much as you can too. Some reliable sources for sports nutrition and training athletes include the following:
  - NCAA Sport Science Institute, which addresses disordered eating, heat and hydration, nutrition, and sleep and wellness.[13]
  - Stacy Sims's book *ROAR*, which addresses female-specific physiology and sports nutrition information.[14]
  - Kathryn E. Ackerman and colleagues' information on relative energy deficiency in sports (RED-S).[15]
  - Team USA and sport-specific national governing bodies (for example, USA Hockey, USRowing, USTA for tennis, etc.).

- Keep in mind that disordered eating often starts unintentionally.[16] Providing education around nutrition, especially specific to sports, can help lay the preventive groundwork.
- Pay attention to the way in which players react to challenges, and keep in mind that something could be off in their diet. While you may be pulling your hair out because someone doesn't seem to be giving their best effort at practice, they might just need a snack.
- Help athletes to understand that caffeine and energy drinks spike mental stimulation and do not provide physical fuel for activity.
- Allow athletes ample time for water breaks during practices and workout sessions. Keep in mind the impacts of the environment and encourage players to stay hydrated throughout the day—not just on game days.

The best part about my mom being my soccer coach is that she loves me. When she blows the whistle and we all talk in a group, she always gives me water. She always keeps me energized and not so sweaty.

—*Tymber, age 7*

- Encourage healthy eating habits and promotion of body positivity. Start by assessing your own feelings, thoughts, behaviors, and language. Modeling is huge when it comes to body positivity.
- Be aware of the messages you convey in casual conversations. Even when you aren't in purposeful discussion about food, eating and body image will surface regularly. Athletes will assume (and rightfully so) that how you talk about your body and food is directly related to how you feel about their bodies and eating behaviors.
- Model intuitive eating and don't discuss the quality of your food as being "bad" or "good" in a nutritional sense. Whether you are making amazing choices yourself or doing what you can at the only fast-food restaurant that is open in town, don't bash your own behaviors.
- Regardless of the sport(s) and gender(s) you coach, be open to conversations and the possibility of disordered eating in athletes. Athletes, by nature, will be more sensitive to body-related issues because they are in the process of striving for excellence. They don't need judgment from their coaches; they need support.

- Do not personally body shame anyone in any way. If you have a habit of physically judging others or yourself, acknowledge that habit, and when it comes up, remind yourself that negative body talk doesn't support anyone's wellness.
- Adopt a no-tolerance policy for food, body, and weight judgments on the team and among athletes. This should discourage comments about anyone and should extend to social media as well.
- Remember that you cannot identify an eating disorder, or lack thereof, by looking at someone.[17]
- Take into consideration the revealing nature of uniforms and team gear. All athletes benefit from feeling confident in their bodies, and their sports gear and equipment should support that as much as possible.
- Silence is communication. If you avoid food- and body-related topics, you may be telling athletes that you do not want to talk about them and/or that you don't care. This will, in turn, encourage their silence as well.
- Help athletes to understand that optimizing physical fitness involves discussion around not just the food we put into our bodies, but other substances as well. Depending upon the level of athletes you coach, you may need to address substance use and abuse. Your stance on illegal drugs should be crystal clear and promote safety and well-being. For drugs that are legal to varying degrees, you must establish clear, consistent policies that you feel comfortable enforcing on a regular basis. Players may be involved in the development of team policies, dependent upon their level of maturity, or they may just need you to establish the boundaries yourself. They need your help in the form of information, guidance, role modeling, and encouragement.
- Teach healthy stress management techniques, encourage sharing feelings, and open the lines of communication. Stress is real, and even the smallest and youngest bodies have to deal with the consequences.
- Advise athletes to prioritize sleep. Athletes tend to be sleep deprived.[18] Their developing brains and hardworking bodies need eight to ten hours each night.
- If you regularly send messages to players, don't message them late at night or early in the morning. Make yourself one fewer person they feel they need to respond to at all hours of the day.
- Explicitly address athletes' need to prioritize sleep as it relates to their use of electronics.

A NOTE ON PREVENTING CHILD ABUSE AND
INTIMATE PARTNER VIOLENCE

One of the hardest parts of teaching and coaching is accepting the harsh reality that many people are victims of a variety of forms of abuse. Keep in mind that not all abuse is physical. Being aware of the signs of abuse is important. If something seems off, there is a chance it is. This is an area in which you will need to consult experts and reach out to others. Whether this information is provided to you or not, be sure you know where to turn when you suspect something is going wrong with an athlete. There are child abuse and intimate partner violence hotlines and reporting procedures that should be followed if you have any inkling that an athlete may be in danger. Hopefully you are just one of many trusted adults looking out for the well-being of the athlete.

The following are some helpful resources:

- If you or someone you know is in immediate need of support, call 1–800–799-SAFE or visit the National Domestic Violence Hotline.[19]
- The U.S. Department of Health and Human Services Children's Bureau works to improve the health and well-being of children and families.[20]
- The National Coalition Against Domestic Violence works to keep people safe, empowered, and free from domestic violence.[21]
- The U.S. Center for SafeSport provides information and trainings for organizations, coaches, parents, and athletes about the prevention of abuse in sports.[22]

APPLICATIONS IN COACH DEVELOPMENT:
SHARING RESOURCES TO HELP COACHES
PROMOTE PHYSICAL WELLNESS

As a coach developer, one of your responsibilities is to help guide coaches to safe practices that are tailored to the age and stage of each athlete.[1] You may be well positioned to bring to light coaching behaviors and other issues that put players' physical wellness at risk. Assisting coaches in employing long-term athlete development and sharing resources that support healthy training regimens, nutrition, and stress management are ways in which coach developers have a real opportunity to improve the wellness of countless athletes. The information coaches need is out there; it just may need to be shared. Athletes see benefits, and coaches can minimize their potential missteps.

At the organizational level, you may be able to suggest the implementation of abuse prevention trainings for coaches (e.g., SafeSport training). At a minimum, where mandatory reporting has not been addressed as a pertinent responsibility of coaches, increasing awareness and providing contact information is essential.

Note
1. Cecile Reynaud, "College and High-Level Amateur Sports," in *Coach Education Essentials: Your Guide to Developing Sport Coaches*, edited by Kristen Dieffenbach and Melissa Thompson (Champaign, IL: Human Kinetics, 2020), 131–54; Matt Robinson, "Athlete Development Process and Coaching," in *Coach Education Essentials: Your Guide to Developing Sport Coaches*, edited by Kristen Dieffenbach and Melissa Thompson (Champaign, IL: Human Kinetics, 2020), 51–66.

STORIES OF *WINNING WELL* IN PHYSICAL WELLNESS

Stories of *Winning Well* are intended to share various perspectives on wellness in sports. The stories remain in the voice of the storyteller to maintain 100 percent authenticity and ownership of their experiences. Real names or pseudonyms are used according to the storyteller's preference. Introductions for each story give you an idea of the source of their perspective; however, that background hardly does justice to their journeys and contributions. While many of the stories address more than one dimension of wellness, the focal point is highlighted while providing an opportunity for your own interpretation of the storyteller's insight.

Susan Francia

Susan Francia fell in love with a sport and pursued it to the ultimate stage. Taking advantage of her natural strength, competitive nature, and tall stature led her to rowing, where she thrived, and everything fell into place. Susan became the top-ranked rower in the world, and she didn't even venture her way into a boat until her sophomore year in college! Her love for the physical feeling of rowing and working with others is visceral and inspiring. Susan's pursuit of her love for the sport along with her coaches' encouragement demonstrate the potential power of striving for physical wellness.

I was 6-foot-2 from the ninth grade on, and being that tall of a woman, I was roped into a lot of different sports. I tried all the tall-person sports—high jump, basketball, etc.—but unfortunately, I was not good. I wanted to be good. I just didn't really have those skill sets, but I still loved being on a team. As proof of that, my senior year in high school, I got one athletic award. It was "Most Spirited." At that point, I had accepted that I probably would not become some sort of great athlete. So when I applied to college, I applied in academics and I ended up going to University of Pennsylvania, in Philly.

My first year at Penn, I was not doing athletics and I ended up not having the structure that I had in high school. Not being part of a team, I had an unbelievable amount of free time and I ended up being the captain of the "Varsity Partying Team." I had a great time but, unfortunately, my grades really suffered. My parents were not happy about that, so they said, "Listen, you need to figure something out because we're not paying for college for you to go and screw around." After that first year, I evaluated what was missing in my life. I knew I missed structure and being part of a team. I figured even if I'm the worst, I'll just try and join some athletic varsity team. I literally looked through a book and saw that rowing was an option, and I had heard that in rowing, again, it was advantageous to be tall. So I went to the first walk-on meeting.

The fall of my sophomore year, I attended that first walk-on meeting even though I had never even picked up an oar in my life. Initially I was very excited, but in the back of my mind I was hesitant, reminding myself that I had been told that I was going to be an all-star basketball player, recruited to college, and that didn't happen. Would rowing also deceive me?

I vividly remember my first rowing practice with the team. The sun was setting over the Philadelphia skyline, and it was a resplendent day to be on the water! I was so captured by my surroundings, in addition to my inexperience, that I unknowingly ended up hitting the girl in front of me in her back with my oar. In rowing it's called a "kidney punch." I kidney punched her, and she was understandably livid. She ended up being one of my best friends afterward, but at the time she turned around and just glared. The reality was, I struggled with rhythm, and I was notorious for hitting people in the back. For the rest of the year, people dreaded sitting in front of me. It wasn't intentional, and I was determined to keep at it because I realized early on that I loved the sport. I was enchanted by the feeling of moving in sync with seven other people and the exhilaration of the speed of the boat as the water rushed past.

The erg (rowing machine) is where I excelled early on. My natural strength and height gave me an advantage to pull numbers that experienced rowers struggled to achieve. My first erg fitness test was one of the best on the whole varsity team. At the time, I didn't even realize that these were tests, and I would pull as hard as I could until my legs and lungs failed me . . . and then I would stop to take a break. I'd grab some water, and the coach would run over exclaiming, "What are you doing?! You have to keep going!" Struggling to catch my breath, I would mumble, "I can't, I need a break. I need some water!" Throughout the year, my breaks got shorter and shorter until finally I figured out that I could power through these workouts. It's funny because if you fast forward to when I went to the Olympics, all my college friends joked, "Don't forget, you can't take a break at the 1,000-meter mark!"

My novice coach at Penn, Scott Belford, was the first person who put the idea of the Olympics into my head. He recognized my physical capabilities and my desire to win. One day after practice, he approached me and remarked, "You know, if you really want this, you could go to the Olympics." I was completely caught off guard; it had never occurred to me. At that moment, I decided that's what I wanted to do. He then said, "If you go to the Olympics, I'm going to be there to watch them put that gold medal around your neck."

Once I started rowing, everything began to fall into place. The intense time commitment helped me find the structure I needed to excel academically, and I ultimately graduated with honors. So my parents were a little surprised when I told them that I was turning down a serious job offer to try out for the Olympic team. They cautioned, "You know, sweetie, you're the 'Most Spirited'; are you sure this is what you want to do?" Without hesitation, I proclaimed, "Absolutely, I love this sport and I know I can be the best in the world!" Fortunately, by that time, I was no longer kidney punching my teammates, my scores were competitive, and I was mentally and physically ready to take the next step.

On the US team, all notions of natural abilities were out the window since everyone else had the exact same stature as me. All of a sudden, it was a level playing field, so it would be up to me to excel among my new teammates. I felt that there was nothing that anyone could say to me to make me excel. It wasn't until I decided that I was willing to push myself to the edge that I finally started to realize my true potential. It was this profound moment where I discovered that in order to excel at this level, I would have to test my ultimate limits.

By the end of my first year training, I successfully made the US World Championship team. I couldn't wait to race with this team that was notorious for sweeping the medal podium. In the final race, it looked like victory was undeniable with a boat length lead at the 1,000-meter mark. Our coxswain motivated us, yelling, "We're on the top of the world!! USA is leading!"—until there were about 500 meters left of the 2,000-meter race and the wheels fell off. We lost by about one foot and we didn't even end up medaling. We went home empty-handed, and it was one of the greatest lessons we could have ever learned.

We thought about that damn race every single practice for the entire following year. It motivated me to hit all my PRs [personal records]. My teammates and I were determined to never lose like that again. Then in 2006, our 8+ came together early on, and our motivation and focus were so in sync that it was just magical. We ended up winning the World Championships that year, leading from start to finish, and even set a new world record. We really connected, and you could feel the energy, knowing that everyone was giving 120 percent. We weren't the strongest crew that I've ever rowed with, but again, we put our hearts and souls on the line from stroke one, and it just clicked. Together we embraced the pain and rode the adrenaline. It was one of those boats that old-timer rowers (which I'm considering myself now) always look back on, thinking that was the pinnacle of good boat feel, just how a boat should run out. I've struggled to find anything that is comparable to that feeling.

Leading into 2008, I had been sitting in the same seat in the 8+ for the previous three years. It was my seat. Except a month before the Olympic selection, our coach sat down the team and announced, "We want to take the fastest boat possible, so everybody will be tested. At this point, I don't know who will be in the eight." And everyone just looked at him like, "What?! What do you mean, you don't know who's going to be in this boat? We know who's going to be in this boat." He said, "Yeah, sorry, we just need to test everyone." So, we were all seat raced.

For a month straight, we showed up to every practice ready to race, switch an athlete, race again, switch again. . . . Coach wanted to find the fastest combination of athletes, and he was going to try every combination possible. On a rare occasion, we had a recovery session, and we did not have to race, but he wouldn't tell us in advance, so mentally we had to prepare to fight for our spot every day. It was the hardest month of my entire life. I'm not joking. At one point, I wanted to quit. It was insanely taxing on all of us, and I felt incredibly relieved when I was finally named to the 2008 Olympic team. Rowing to the starting line of my first Olympic race, I wondered why I wasn't more nervous or jittery. Out in the middle of the Beijing rowing course, I suddenly realized all those seat races instilled in me the confidence in my own abilities and the confidence in my teammates. I thought, "Oh that's why we just went to hell and back. So that when I sit on this starting line, I'm ready."

I still remember the race and how much we were in tune with one another. The energy and excitement propelled us to get our boat out in front to an early lead. This time when our coxswain exclaimed, "We're on top of the world!" we stayed on top of the world. With ten strokes left, we were a boat length up, and I just knew the victory was ours. I peeked out of the boat right as we crossed the finish line, thinking, "Holy shit! I just won a gold medal!" Coach Belford was there to see them put that gold medal around my neck.

Coming down from the glory of the Olympics was challenging and I wasn't sure what I would do next. It sounds kind of corny, but going out for that first row two months after the Olympics was such a beautiful feeling. I was rowing alone in the single, but for the first time in weeks, I felt an insane joy. In those few months, I rediscovered my passion for the sport. I loved it.

Of course, leading into 2012 was going to be a different ball game. At that point, I was back in the flagship boat, the 8+. We had won six consecutive World Championship titles, and with the addition of that Olympic gold in 2008, we were no longer the underdog. We were now the ones with a big target on our back. 2012 was going to be an interesting year.

The expectations from the outside had changed, but internally, we were motivated as ever. There were only a few different athletes from our 2008 boat, but what those new athletes lacked in experience, they more than made up for in physical power and enthusiasm. The London boat was incredibly strong. I'll never forget our starting strokes; it felt like a rocket launch. I had never felt so confident that we would win. We led the race from start to finish, and, this time, our coxswain didn't need to tell me we were on top of the world. I already knew. Winning gold the second time felt just as amazing. When they put that medal around my neck, I cried, just like the first time.

In 2014, I officially retired from the US team, but I really wanted to give back to the sport that had changed my life. I decided to start coaching at the San Diego Rowing Club. Coaching gave me a new purpose and ability to share my love of the sport. Who knows . . . perhaps one day one of my athletes will be on the Olympic podium as I cheer from the stands.

Rick Howard

Rick Howard is an expert in long-term athlete development, a model originally established to help athletes reach their potential, specifically in the physical realm, although it has expanded since. He is well respected in the coach development world and has led many efforts to improve sport at all levels. He has worked extensively with the National Strength and Conditioning

Association and is a professor of applied sport science at West Chester University. To complement his emphasis on physical wellness, Rick maintains a strong commitment to helping coaches develop the whole athlete.

Long-term athlete development is a framework that shapes a child-centered and parent-supported coaching philosophy. LTAD recognizes that all of us are athletes—it exists from cradle to grave. It helps coaches engage kids of all ages in developmentally appropriate games, sports, and activities, that lead them to a healthful journey of being active across the life span.

While much of LTAD focuses on physical development, it also recognizes that we play a huge role in the lives of our athletes that transcends sports! We have the opportunity to help develop the whole child, not just the physical child. The central tenet of all long-term athletic development programs is the health and well-being of the child. Not winning! Not just the physical.

Most coaches focus on what we know—the physical dimension of our craft, the technical and tactical skills necessary to play the game and the physical training needed to improve those skills. We might even consider "mental" skills like mental toughness, but breaking down kids or having them work beyond fatigue is counterproductive to their physical development.

To truly develop the health and well-being of every child, coaches should consider guiding their athletes to develop all eight dimensions of wellness (yes, the physical dimension is an important dimension, but it is not the only one) to create holistic positive youth development. Give kids choices, develop them as leaders (not just the team captains), and involve kids in decisions, for starters. How coaches balance all dimensions of wellness leads to health and well-being because if one dimension is deflated, the whole wellness wheel is flat! So just as coaches are intentional with practice plans to develop the physical dimension of athletes, they should take time to proactively include activities, challenges, and conversations to develop their whole being!

2

Social Wellness

People don't care how much you know until they know how much you care.

—*Theodore Roosevelt*

A common mistake among those who work in sport is spending a disproportional amount of time on "Xs and Os" as compared to time spent learning about people.

—*Mike Krzyzewski*

WHAT IS SOCIAL WELLNESS IN THE CONTEXT OF SPORTS?

Humans are innately social beings. Whether we consider ourselves to be introverts or extroverts, modern times are characterized by social humanity, and we are interacting with one another constantly. Social wellness is a complicated beast. According to Student Health and Counseling Services at the University of California, Davis, it "involves building healthy, nurturing and supportive relationships as well as fostering a genuine connection with those around you."[1] This dimension can get messy for sure, and it can also be incredibly rewarding, meaningful, and inspiring. The connections we build with others serve as a priority in our lives, and sports provide a natural breeding ground for connection. We all have and need relationships, and helping athletes to foster positive interactions is one of our many essential roles as coaches.

WHY DOES SOCIAL WELLNESS MATTER IN THE WORLD OF ATHLETICS?

Social connection is essential for our physiological, emotional, and psychological well-being.[2] We are wired for connection, and that connection has legitimate impacts on our quality of life, including our overall health.

Coaches often hear about the importance of building relationships with players and others with whom they work. Quality connections are an essential component to success.[3] While we don't always know the best way to go about the process of building bridges with every single person we meet, there is no denying the power of authentic connection. In strong leadership, there is a clearly communicated concern for others.[4] When such bonds are built between coaches and athletes, the results can be extremely powerful. You may have heard that "so-and-so would go to the ends of the earth for their coach" or that "those players would run through a brick wall for their coach." There is something special about the bonds that are built in sports and particularly those between athletes and coaches—they are central to the experience.

According to Peter Senge, successful teams are ultimately powerful and are built on the relationships between each of their members.[5] When strong connections exist, people conjure up strength they never knew they had and realize success they never thought possible. This is the glory of our social nature—it has the potential to impact us at a level that is almost impossible to describe but is innately understood. When we are in a group and things are working, everyone is playing their role to the best of their ability and the shared purpose is clear, we bring out the best in one another.

Coming together as a group of unique individuals in a concerted effort is something we can experience in many places in life; however, there is something magical about those efforts on sports teams. Even if you coach just one athlete in an individual sport, the two of you are a team. There will always be opportunities for people to work together in sports, and the better we do with the social aspect of athletics, the more likely we are to bring home the Ws.

PROBLEM: WE CAN'T TEXT EACH OTHER THE PLAN MIDGAME!

With increasing ability to communicate with one another from behind a screen, the quantity and quality of in-person connections may be at risk.

Unless the face of sports changes dramatically (outside of eSports), there will always be people, in their truest form, without devices, playing. As long as that is the case, social wellness will continue to play a central role in the sports experience for all of us.

A NOTE ON FEASIBILITY AS IT RELATES TO SOCIAL WELLNESS

In relation to maximizing social wellness, a few barriers that you may encounter include, but are not limited to, the following:

- Varied cultural differences and expectations around communication and relationships may surface in relation to coach-athlete, athlete-athlete, or coach-parent interactions.
- Language barriers arise with written materials and verbally shared information.
- Not all communication channels are accessible to all athletes and families.
- There may be financial and logistical barriers to formal and informal team bonding activities.
- Athletes' personal comfort zones will vary in relation to team-building efforts.
- All team members will be on a journey to learn about one another and each person's understanding, education, and experiences with other cultures will influence their interactions.
- Different aspects of athletes' identities may impact their real or perceived safety and/or support in social groups.
- Some athletes may display deeply entrenched social behaviors that they have adapted to protect themselves (such as minimizing eye contact, avoiding physical proximity, or acting as a "class clown").
- We all communicate through our identities, consciously and subconsciously. We cannot separate who we are from our experience and neither can others.

While this list is not exhaustive, taking the time to acknowledge potential barriers to wellness is imperative.

Social wellness in sports supports interpersonal connection and positive interactions with others, supportive coach–athlete relationships, cohesion among team members, and helpful interactions with parents, officials, opponents, and others.

WHERE ARE YOU NOW?

1. How do you feel about your current social wellness?
2. How do you feel about the social wellness of the athletes you coach?
3. How much of a priority is it for you to support your athletes' social wellness?
4. How well-informed and prepared do you feel to help maximize social wellness in the athletes you coach?
5. How do your personal and coaching practices support or detract from your athletes' social wellness?

TIPS FOR SUPPORTING YOUR OWN SOCIAL WELLNESS

We can't just drop our personal social lives to be on the sidelines with athletes and expect to maintain wellness. As a coach, you owe it to yourself, your athletes, and everyone in your life to prioritize the connections that *you* value and to foster and model healthy interactions with others. Specific to team dynamics and the relationships that you build on the coaching staff and with athletes, consider the following:

- First of all, athletes don't need you to be their friend, or vice versa. They need you to be a trusted, caring adult. They need a leader, and you need to maintain your boundaries. This is not just about professionalism (although that is a part of it); it also helps ensure the establishment of authentic, respectable relationships built on a foundation of trust.
- Build an authentic, supportive coaching staff and network. Your support can come from inside the coaching world or out, within your sport or across sports, and from any level or location. We all need to be able to share the experience with someone who recognizes our common ground and can empathize.[6]

- A strong coaching staff works through challenging times and has fun together. They may disagree from time to time, but when they take their message to the team, it is with one voice. They are, in essence, a team as well.
- Ensure that the relationships in your world outside of coaching get a break from your sport. Friends and family don't need all your interactions to revolve around coaching.
- Players should never hear you venting about other players, fellow coaches should never hear your griping about someone else on staff. It may sound juvenile, but in the heat of the moment (which can comprise much of a sports season), think before you speak so that you can maintain the best relationships possible, both inside and outside your sport.

TIPS FOR SUPPORTING ATHLETES' SOCIAL WELLNESS

Players will look to you for guidance in multiple facets of their social lives. They will seek your approval in many ways and hope for a positive connection. They will emulate your leadership practices and, in particular, your treatment of others. Show them how to remain focused on a goal while valuing all the people striving to reach that goal.

I love that sports bring people together. During high school volleyball season, I knew that I would see familiar faces cheering my team on from the stands no matter where I was playing. On my team there were plenty of girls I never would have had the chance to meet if it weren't for volleyball.

—*Stella, age 18*

Athletes should be able to count on you to genuinely care about their need to fit in, feel supported, and build safe relationships with others. The following are some suggestions for supporting their social wellness:

- Build a safe, supportive community for all players and coaches, making your expectations for interpersonal communication clear. Guide players to support one another as unique individuals, and allow space for genuine connections to form, laying the groundwork for inclusion in your program and in life.
- As a role model, focus on empathy in all of your interactions. Provide an ideal example for athletes in terms of communicating with teammates,

opponents, and officials. Players will emulate your communication—healthy and unhealthy, and pertaining to interactions on and off the field of play.

- Give players direct instruction on how you want them to communicate with one another during practices and competitions. Consider allowing only supportive comments between athletes at all times. Their role is to encourage one another, not to coach. You will need to explicitly teach this to athletes, model it, address it regularly, and highlight its value within the scope of the game and beyond.

- Explicitly address safe, productive relationships and what that means in any context. Let players know that any relationship that is unsafe is not okay and provide them with resources to help them mitigate harmful situations.

- Get to know your players as people outside of your sport. Use the time you have before and after practices and on road trips to learn more about athletes' interests, hobbies, and backgrounds. If possible, attend a concert, a play, or another sporting event to show your support for them as a person.

- Establish trust by holding players accountable. We all crave structure and responsibility. You may have to provide ample support in helping athletes to follow through with their accountability in sports because it may not be an emphasis anywhere else in their world. Accountability is built on consistent expectations and a lot of hard work and investment in people.[7]

- Use an equity lens in all decisions and continue to do as much personal growth in this area as possible. Recognize systems of oppression and opportunities for accommodations. More than anything, listen.

- Provide written and verbal communication in the language that is best for each family and athlete, incorporating translators as needed.

- Have players share their gender pronouns and preferred names.

- Avoid gendered language when addressing groups, in an effort to be inclusive. For example, terms such as "boys," "ladies," or "guys" can be replaced with "everyone," "you all," or "people."

- Make space for athletes to share cultural experiences and traditions as much as they would like. Do not single out or tokenize anyone and ensure players don't feel like they are being forced to share.

- Some coaches will talk about teams as families, which is effective if there is a clear understanding of what "family" means. Telling some players that the team is a family may bring up painful experiences and/or trauma.

- Team building, approached from a social wellness perspective, is focused on establishing healthy, supportive connections. The following are a few tips to consider in those times of bonding:
  - Establish and maintain guidelines around confidentiality.
  - Set up activities to allow individuals to engage at the level at which they are comfortable and to do so without judgment from others.
  - Emphasize safety and support.
  - Teach athletes to listen wholeheartedly to the stories of others without building comparisons. When someone is sharing, the job of others is simply to listen, learn, and support.
  - Encourage players to share difficulties as well as successes with one another.
  - Encourage players to connect outside of the sport. Remind them to take the time to appreciate the entire experience of their teammates' lives.
  - Help support players in challenging their biases and preconceived notions of others. Much of this can be done through modeling.
  - Show enthusiasm for the fun that players have together and embrace that energy. It is often the people and the fun times that we remember long after the games have ended.

MANAGING SOCIAL MEDIA IN SPORTS

In addition to a constantly evolving social media landscape (new apps, increased access to video, more or less dependency on digital communication, future regulations, etc.), managing social media in sports is complicated by the level to which people depend on constant feedback and want to share their personal experiences. We have to find a balance and reinforce healthy boundaries with athletes. Just as we need their perspective and input, they often need our guidance and structure.[8] There can be negative consequences to what people see and experience online. On the other hand, social media provides a platform for viewing competitions and magnifying positive sports news. There is increased space for social connection and valuable dialogue among teammates, friends, and family.

In the midst of a season, athletes work to establish and clarify their identity within the sport, including their individual capabilities and value to the team. Social media often serves as a place to quickly find opinions, critiques, and naysayers who may destroy an athlete's self-esteem. To help mitigate the challenges associated with social media in sports, determine how it fits into your coaching philosophy, guide your players in appropriate use, and follow through with your expectations as a staff. Promote the healthy side of technology's influence and steer your players away from harming themselves or others online. The more openly we address the pros and cons of social media and instant gratification, the more effectively we can use technology.

FORMING A PARTNERSHIP WITH PARENTS

Families are unique and all athletes will have their own version of a support system—or, unfortunately, lack thereof. Throughout this book, the word "parent" refers to those people who care for athletes. They may be a legal guardian or something completely different.

Variability from one family to the next is important to keep in mind throughout the season. When there is a parent meeting, snack rotation, or recognition ceremony of some sort, be aware of and sensitive to the diversity of families with whom you work. Be cognizant of the language you use and how it may be perceived. For example, instead of "Moms' Night," consider "Fans' Night," to be more inclusive. Offer alternative meeting times and locations as well as translated materials to fit all families' needs. Inclusion should be your priority, and there may be some fun adjustments you can make in your plans and/or messaging to ensure that everyone feels welcomed.

While collaborating with parents can be an extremely challenging aspect of coaching, it can also be a very rewarding and powerful part of your work. As Daniel Gould and Jenny Nalepa explain, "As a coach, avoiding athletes' parents is a grave mistake. First, the majority of sport parents, as supported by the literature, do not cause problems and do provide logistical and social-emotional support to their children as well as support program goals."[9]

Working with parents can be a source of heightened emotions combined with sticky logistics. They bring an additional level of complexity because they, too, are human. Parents will engage at different levels and it is important to avoid assuming the best or the worst with any of them—even from one season to the next. The following are a few ideas to consider when forming a partnership with parents:

- Before anything else, determine where you and the parents share common ground so that you can guide your efforts toward a partnership.

- Julie McCleery recommends creating an Athlete's Bill of Rights to ensure that parents and coaches are on the same page.[10] This decree should focus on athlete safety and efforts that can be taken jointly to help the athletes thrive in their sports environment. As she explains, you may want to involve parents' and/or players' input in the creation of the Athlete's Bill of Rights.

- When approaching a meeting with a group of parents or individuals, be sure to consider and value their perspective as an essential component in the process. Awareness of alternative viewpoints is always helpful and can serve an important role in solidifying the decisions you make.

- Hold a parent meeting at the beginning of the season and clearly define the role of parents in the program. Some might be new to the sports parenting world, some may be new to you and your philosophy, and some may have been around you for years and need to know what it is you hope for in the current season. Share a bit of your philosophy and highlight your shared interest in athlete safety and a positive experience. Be sure to address your expectations and ways for parents to get involved and/or help. This is a crucial step in building relationships with parents.

- Build positive relationships with parents and maintain your boundaries. When a difficult situation arises, approach it as you would a conflict with a coworker. Respect the roles that each of you maintains. Be friendly, smile, and be yourself. Don't get caught up in a trap of going outside your philosophy and beliefs to appease a parent. Be thoughtful, empathetic, and firm with your words and actions.

- Communicate team values and accomplishments consistently. Not only will this help you to build and reinforce the culture you want to support in your team, it serves to keep parents involved at the level that you desire. If you want that communication to be one-way, there are specific apps available that will allow you to send messages without the option for others to reply.

- Keep in mind that you are the only one with your perspective. You create the practice plans, you lead team meetings, and you have many conversations with players. When you make an effort to coach the whole person and you do so with integrity, you have nothing to be ashamed of. There will always be different ways to coach a game or sport. Choose the one that works for you and who you are, and be confident. A parent may or may not understand your perspective, or you theirs, but that is okay. You have very different roles. Do your best to have compassion for where they are coming from.

APPLICATIONS IN COACH DEVELOPMENT: FOSTERING PRODUCTIVE RELATIONSHIPS WITH COACHES AND COACHES' HEALTHY CONNECTIONS WITH ATHLETES AND FAMILIES

As you address the pillars of successful coaching, remember the integral role played by your relationships with coaches. Your connection with a coach will help to maximize coach development efforts and may also serve as a model for their relationships with athletes and families. In terms of improving coaching, your empathy and support may be just as impactful, if not more, than your expertise. To help them realize their full potential, coaches will need to solidify their values and priorities, identify their strengths and weaknesses, and authentically embrace their own learning process. This demands a strong interpersonal connection between the coach and coach developer.[1] The subject matter within which you are working may be coaching sports, but the recipients of your targeted learning are the coaches—connect with them.

As a coach developer, you are well-positioned to help coaches navigate and establish appropriate relationships. Dependent upon the age and stage of the athletes, the coach-athlete relationship will take on a variety of characteristics, yet demonstrating integrity and prioritizing safety for all athletes should be at the forefront of all coach-athlete interactions.[2] In some cases, blatant abuse occurs, and a coach developer must serve as a safety net to help protect athletes. There are other questionable interactions that incite much less dangerous consequences for the athlete and/or coach but can nonetheless destroy a coach's reputation and undermine the integrity of the profession. Sports provide a breeding ground for authenticity and collaboration and, as a result, the potential for deep personal relationships. Even coaches with the best intentions and highest moral standards may need your help in establishing clear boundaries. It is also important to help coaches recognize when they may be construed as favoring a particular family, isolating a specific family, or resisting interaction with parents and/or families in general. When engaging with families the risk of abusing the power dynamic and/or muddying the waters with a minor is less prevalent; however, the potential to create conflict and mistrust among all families in the program is high. It may take a lot of courage and compassion on your part to effectively discuss relationship boundaries with a coach, but that difficult conversation may be one of the most important you have with a mentee. Helping coaches to maintain their integrity should serve as a basic tenet of coach development programming.

Collaborating effectively with families can be one of the most difficult aspects of coaching, especially for a novice coach. Parents don't need to be in control of the program, but their well-defined role as partners may prove invaluable for athletes and coaches alike.[3] While it is true that many families are helpful in the sports experience, just one negative interaction can put a coach on edge for quite some time. Specific to the coaching context, and as appropriate, do your part to help coaches build connections with athletes' families. This is an area in which you will get to showcase your support and encouragement for a coach's philosophy, values, communication skills, and confidence. The interactions that coaches have with parents are one of the major reasons coaches step away from the game,[4] and if it is possible to salvage the situation for everyone involved, a coach developer may be in a perfect position to do so.

Notes

1. Sarah McQuade, "Current Models of Coach Education, Training, and Certification," in *Coach Education Essentials: Your Guide to Developing Sport Coaches*, edited by Kristen Dieffenbach and Melissa Thompson (Champaign, IL: Human Kinetics, 2020), 187–208; François Rodrigue, and Pierre Trudel, "A 'Personal Learning Coach' for High-Performance Coaches," in *Coach Education and Development in Sport: Instructional Strategies*, edited by Bettina Callary and Brian Gearity (New York: Routledge, 2020), 141–53.

2. U.S. Center for SafeSport, https://uscenterforsafesport.org/.

3. Julie McCleery, "Dr. Julie McCleery: Building Bridges with Parents," produced by Center for Leadership in Athletics, University of Washington, Ambitious Coaching Podcast, fall 2018, https://soundcloud.com/user-617023187/building_bridges_launch_version.

4. Charlie Miller, "Syracuse.com Survey: Parents, You're Driving High School Coaches Crazy," Syracuse.com, May 23, 2019, https://www.syracuse.com/sports/2016/09/syracusecom_survey_parents_youre_driving_high_school_coaches_crazy.html#incart_river_index.

STORIES OF *WINNING WELL* IN SOCIAL WELLNESS

Kiauna Floyd

Kiauna Floyd is a restaurant owner in Portland, Oregon—no small feat in a city that is known as a destination for foodies. She earned Hall of Fame honors at her high school and continued on to become an All-American athlete at Portland State University. Kiauna has a dynamic personality and has grown into a thriving and confident leader. The social wellness she was able to nurture in sports, supported by authentic relationships with her coaches, has contributed greatly to her success and happiness.

I have been a competitor since I can remember. It began with a love for all physical activities and landed me on the softball field. There are pictures of me as an infant in the arms of my parents' teammates starting when I was a few weeks old. I have the same kind of pictures of my kids, as little babies, with a ball in their tiny hands. Sports, being such a huge part of my journey, have continued through each chapter of my existence and still do.

Owning a restaurant during COVID-19 challenged my resolve and inner strength. It was probably the hardest, most challenging time in business that I have ever faced. Although the unprecedented times afforded us no user manual, failure was not an option. Being an athlete is the foundation of my competitive nature and resilience. It fueled my ability to pivot, innovate, and execute through adversity. As a business owner, I know how to lead, communicate, set goals, and succeed with others and most of all, I know how to have fun. My Amalfi's team and I are one big family. In the restaurant industry, a busy evening on a busy weekend is a lot like playing in a tournament, except now I'm the coach.

I think that any serious competitor misses their sport immensely. There's never been a time in my life that I haven't missed playing. I appreciated the simplicity of working hard and seeing results on the scoreboard and in the record books. I enjoyed the physicality and seeing all my efforts come to fruition after months and months of training. One of the most impactful aspects of sports for me was the relationship building and social component.

Some of my best friendships derived from sports and going into battle with my teammates. We can go days, months, years without seeing each other and then when we reconnect, it is the deepest, most genuine, heartfelt connection a person can feel. I think it is because we were on the field together, and you just get to know people in the most vulnerable ways. I don't know what else gives you this feeling, other than maybe the armed forces. This level of relationship is hard to understand if you haven't been there. For me, it's a bond born out of sports. For example, my husband is also an athlete. The connection we have and the family we have built is much like the teams we have both played on. We work hard to perfect our contributions to the team. We do what we need to do to overcome challenges. We strive for greatness and pass it on to our children.

The connection I had with my coaches also had a huge impact on me. I was fortunate to have had the guidance of many great coaches throughout my athletic career, and even more fortunate that the majority were fierce women who previously played the sport they coached. They knew all aspects of the game, which gave me a sense of confidence and unwavering trust in their decision-making. Everything they asked me to do, I knew they, too, had done at some point in their career. In return, I gave maximum effort to all things asked of me. Having this symbiotic relationship with your coach is very special.

Being a Black softball player in a mostly white sport (at the time) presented a unique experience. There were times where I observed certain behaviors or heard comments that were degrading and stereotypical to my people, although not often directed toward me. It was like I was looked at differently, yet it still stung. On the other hand, sports provided the one place I could go and feel included and equal. Every softball team I played for, from Little League to college, I was always the only girl of color. For me, it felt powerful. I was breaking ground. Sports gave me a special identity. However, as a young biracial girl, I felt pressures at every turn to pick and choose one side or the other (*Are you black or white?*). I never had to do that in sports. I could be me. Being the only player of color was of no importance or concern for any of my teammates or coaches. Teammates share a camaraderie and bond which parallels family.

The ladies I played ball with were my sisters. They had my back and I, theirs—on and off the battlefield. It's hard to put into words the strength and complexity of that bond.

Robin Selvig

The University of Montana women's basketball program built a tradition unlike many others in the history of college basketball led by Coach Robin Selvig, who finished his career with 865 wins. Fueled by a focus on the social wellness of his teams, Rob and the Lady Griz program earned respect nationwide. If you ask him about his career, the memories, or what he misses in retirement, he will authentically express his deep gratitude for the relationships and the people that make up the Lady Griz family.

I have a hard time talking about me and my role in all of this because anything that "I" accomplished, I never did alone. There are just so many people involved in it. Things worked out pretty well for us, and it wasn't because of some grand scheme or plan I came up with.

From the beginning of my career, I was fortunate because I got in at the start of women's sports. Being a part of all that was very rewarding. We weren't just experiencing it here, but it was everywhere. I had never looked at coaching men or women any differently, and I wouldn't have done it any differently. I have great respect for women as athletes—they sometimes worked even harder because they had something to prove due to the fact this was all just starting for them. My players were an inspiration to me, and they continue to be today.

Regardless of the outcome of the game, I was going to win or lose with the team. It wasn't about me at all, but I was going to do everything I could to help the ladies win. I'd feel bad when we didn't win because I always wanted that for them, but we could be proud of ourselves if we gave our best, no matter what. And ultimately, it was really all about the team and about the connections we had with each other.

When I first started coaching, I just did it because I loved the game. I liked being around the kids, and I was gonna coach the best I could. I thought it was important that the players recognized that each year mattered, and each team was different. They didn't have to live up to anything specific to me. We just had to do the best that we could. It was refreshing and exciting, and we happened to have a lot of success with those teams. When you have a healthy team, they all pull for each other—they make the most of what you've got. Once we were an established program, the younger kids learned from the older kids, and what they expected of each other became really clear. There were more important things than just basketball going on all the time. Being on a team and enjoying a team, that's what it's all about. With all the expectations out there now, for kids to enjoy playing can be hard, and it shouldn't be that way.

Even though the individual stuff was never my focus, one of the hardest parts of coaching for me was that it didn't always work out exactly as every player wanted it to on an individual level. It couldn't. That's just not possible. Not everyone gets to be a starter or the star, and I have great empathy for the players who didn't get to have it go exactly as they had hoped. All I could do is what I thought was best, and I'm not always right all the time. I felt terrible after games when people didn't get to play. I wanted to make everybody happy, and that part was really hard for me. Even though not everyone could be the star, I wanted everybody to know they were of great importance to the team and how the team performed, and I talked about that all the time. I wanted to make sure that everyone knew they were a part of this, and the basketball mattered, but there was always just so much more to it. Things turned out pretty good for us, not because of some big system I had set up, but because of how I felt about the players. They knew that I cared.

I remember talking to players in my office and telling them to not let basketball be their identity. Everyone on the team was so much more than just a basketball player or athlete. That can be really tough for people to understand, especially nowadays, with players competing on club teams year-round, but it's true. Basketball is just a game, and it's a great game—it should be fun. But it's just a game. There is so much more to life. So, we would talk about that, and that's where the relationships come in.

What makes all of this meaningful is the fact that we get to share it with one another. Individual sports are great, but doing things as a team, for me, is what makes it special. The things that you share are not just wins and losses. You share experiences that are important in life—the ups and downs. Those are the things you remember. You win a championship, and when you share it with people, that's what makes it meaningful. Being on a team and part of a team (whether you are a coach or player) is pretty incredible. It's something that is hard to explain if you haven't been a part of it.

When I retired, there was a party for me that I expected to be fun, but I never expected it to be half as big as it was. Not all the players could make it, but almost every single player who had been a part of the program in those thirty-eight years [when I was coaching] made it there. I was blown away by the turnout. That was as meaningful to me as anything that happened in my coaching years. To be able to see the Lady Griz family together and to see everyone sharing the things they had in common, from the youngest players to the oldest, was really special. To be there and realize that we all shared that stuff, and it wasn't just all about winning championships. Hearing athletes tell stories about how they were there for each other and they still are—that was the best part. It means the world to me because that was my life. I have lifelong friendships from it and connections with so many players.

In retirement, I miss the everyday interactions with the athletes, and I don't really miss much of anything else. It was a great run for me, I have no complaints about it, but I do miss joking around with players. I miss sharing the ups and downs with them and with my assistants. All my assistants played for me, and so for years we shared a lot together. They were with me for a long time, which was great. It was a great thing for me—I had people assisting me who could try and understand me and knew me well enough to be able to. When I talk about sharing, they are all a part of it. People had babies, life happened, and we were all a part of each other's lives and families. I loved coaching, and to me it always has been and still is about the people and the connections and relationships.

3

Emotional Wellness

I've learned that people will forget what you said, people will forget what you did, but people will never forget how you made them feel.

—*Maya Angelou*

WHAT IS EMOTIONAL WELLNESS IN THE CONTEXT OF SPORTS?

The term "emotional wellness" is used interchangeably with "mental health," and mental health is a *huge* issue in today's society. Sports are not immune to such issues. Although coaches are not expected to have all the answers, it is our duty to be informed, serve as allies, and consult experts as needed. We are key members on the support teams of the athletes we coach. Getting to know athletes as we do places us in an excellent position to help. Players' lives literally depend on it.

Emotional wellness is about recognizing emotions, connecting with them, allowing them to exist, and managing associated behaviors to the best of our abilities. It is normal for people to assume that being emotionally well means either feeling happy all day long or "controlling" one's emotions. The truth is that neither of those scenarios would likely be described as "healthy." When something tragic happens in the world, feeling sad or upset is appropriate and should be supported. Trying to control such emotions is one of many factors that has warped cultural norms. To be whole and to be true to ourselves, we need to embrace the good, the bad, and the ugly without judging those

35

emotions as such. Locking any of that up is extremely detrimental and can lead to a variety of negative outcomes.

Because sports act as a microcosm of society,[1] we bring many unhealthy cultural practices around emotional wellness directly to the playing field. In addition to our culturally influenced muting of emotions, we need to consider the heightened feelings often associated with competition and sports. In athletics, just as in life, emotional wellness is about how we recognize, experience, and express our feelings. Emotional wellness in the sports scene involves recognizing the whole person in each athlete as well as facilitating the management of all of sports' ups and downs.

WHY DOES EMOTIONAL WELLNESS MATTER IN THE WORLD OF ATHLETICS?

Our primary motivators—in all things—are emotions.[2] Emotions cannot be shut off or removed, and we need to work with them. As athletes and coaches, there is a disconnect in this area. Many emotions are frowned upon in sport culture, and we need to turn the tide. Lori Gottlieb explains the current state of emotional wellness very clearly, stating, "No matter how open we as a society are about formerly private matters, the stigma around our emotional struggles remains formidable."[3] In the world of sports, can we have the chance to be bummed for a bit? Conversely, can we celebrate the success of a team and cry tears of joy and satisfaction? Or do we have to maintain a robot-like stoic attitude because we're so tough? The concept is absurd, not to mention inauthentic and emotionally stunting.

While we may not give emotional wellness the attention it's due, the impact it can have on other aspects of life seems to be more accepted or understood than is the case for the other dimensions of wellness. If things are falling apart for you emotionally, you will likely start to struggle in other realms as well. There is, however, a powerful upside to all of this. When we feel our feelings (both comfortable and uncomfortable ones), we allow ourselves to be whole.[4] With our emotions in hand, we can jump into relationships with others and challenges of all varieties with strength and conviction. We can bring that driving force with us onto our teams. We eliminate the need to hide and hold ourselves back while simultaneously allowing ourselves the freedom to give our best. Emotional wellness builds a safety net for each of us that doesn't tell us everything is going to be perfect all the time, but that whatever is, will be. Letting go of our preconceived notions about what's "good" or "bad" in terms of emotions is a key factor in providing the opportunity for us to truly be present, let go of damaging pressures, and play.

The goal is to be as competitive as possible while purposefully channeling all that emotional energy. It is no secret that athletes who are driven by something emotionally are more willing to put in the extra effort, to push harder, and to passionately fight for a win. In addition to all the benefits one sees as a result of investing in emotional wellness, more fierce competition and resulting success on the court, track, field or ice go hand in hand. Playing with emotion is a good thing. We need it if we want to bring home the trophies.

PROBLEM: WE AREN'T COACHING ROBOTS— THESE HUMANS HAVE FEELINGS!

As a society, we have taught generations of athletes to believe that being tough is about being unemotional. Coaches strive to cultivate "mental toughness" (determination, perseverance, and drive to be specific), but when it comes to emotions, the plan to cover them up, push them aside, and "tough it out" is not productive. There is no doubt that toxic masculinity has negatively impacted society as a whole along with persons of all genders.[5] The idea that "there is no crying in baseball," as expressed by Tom Hanks in *A League of Their Own*, demonstrates such unrealistic expectations.[6] Masculinity or "toughness" that mutes emotions is inhumane and harmful, and increases the prevalence of suicide.[7] Sports have, unfortunately, provided a breeding ground for such detrimental practices.

Many courageous athletes and leaders are working to reveal the lack of emotional wellness in athletics; however, we have *barely* skimmed the surface as an industry. Mental health is a core component of cultures of excellence,[8] yet what we actually see in many competitive environments tells a very different story. After being entrenched in a sports system characterized by a harmful practice of emotional avoidance, Kevin Love spoke out, saying, "Everyone is going through something that we can't see. Mental health is an invisible thing, but it touches us at some point or another."[9] His honesty and vulnerability opened the doors to conversations around emotional struggles of athletes on and off the field of play.

A cultural shift is needed to remove the stigma around reaching out for help. Most coaches are not trained therapists. In relation to our emotional wellness as well as that of our athletes, there are efforts we can make on our own to support healthy behaviors and there are also times when the help of a professional is absolutely necessary. This is as true for coaches as it is for athletes.

A NOTE ON FEASIBILITY AS IT RELATES TO EMOTIONAL WELLNESS

In relation to maximizing emotional wellness, a few barriers that you may encounter include, but are not limited to, the following:

- Emotional intelligence and capacity vary greatly among athletes, even within the same age group.
- Trauma may play a major role in athletes' lives and is not something we can easily predict or identify on the surface.
- Emotional wellness across the board may be stunted. Mainstream culture does not generally support expression of raw emotions and productive coping mechanisms.
- Empathy is an emotional process that may take considerable effort over time. Connecting with the emotional experience of another person requires an openness to one's own emotions and experiences.

While this list is not exhaustive, taking the time to acknowledge potential barriers to wellness is imperative.

Emotional wellness in sports recognizes the importance of emotions and managing them to cope effectively with life and performance demands, supports the expression of emotions, provides a safe environment for all athletes, prioritizes healthy stress management, and promotes joy.

WHERE ARE YOU NOW?

1. How do you feel about your current emotional wellness?
2. How do you feel about the emotional wellness of the athletes you coach?
3. How much of a priority is it for you to support your athletes' emotional wellness?

4. How well-informed and prepared do you feel to help maximize emotional wellness in the athletes you coach?

5. How do your personal and coaching practices support or detract from your athletes' emotional wellness?

TIPS FOR SUPPORTING YOUR OWN EMOTIONAL WELLNESS

The following are a few ideas for you to counteract the stigma around emotional wellness:

- Be a human first and a coach second. It can be easy to get caught up in all the excitement and lose sight of who you are as a person. If you find yourself getting wrapped up in the idea that your sport is life, take a step back and check your reality.

- If you are at home with your family, be at home with your family. Unprocessed emotions and coaching stress can distract you from your personal life and priorities. Be honest with your family about the season but avoid making your sport the entire family's life. Find out how involved they want to be in this process with you and respect those boundaries. Don't forget that they are likely some of your biggest supporters.

- Practice mindfulness (for advice and tips, Headspace is a good place to start).[10] When you focus your energy in the present as opposed to the past or future, you can grant each moment the attention it deserves. Sports provide ample opportunities for practicing mindfulness in the moments that we find ourselves 100 percent focused on the game. Applying that same level of focus to anything else (our breathing, environment, or emotions, for example) while minimizing other distractions (other people, cell phones, etc.) is what allows us to be present. Even a momentary break from the hectic pace of life is helpful and can lower stress levels. Identify the times you need a break and go for it. There is really no right or wrong way of "doing" mindfulness.

- Hard times allow coaches to be vulnerable, to heal, to learn, and to move on stronger than before.[11]

- Bottling up our emotions will not work, and sharing our coaching frustrations with the wrong crowd (athletes, parents, etc.) isn't helpful either. It can be easy to vent to a newspaper reporter, for example, but before you do so, think about the potential consequences.

- Remember that there is no shame in asking for and/or seeking help and support. Emotions can be incredibly challenging and truthfully, acknowledging emotions and recognizing the need to reach out for help is one of the strongest, bravest, most admirable moves a person can make.
- If feasible, see a mental health professional regularly, even if you don't feel like you are in crisis.

I love being in sports. It is a great way to get anger out and get your anger out in a good way. I love all my coaches so much. They have made such a huge impact on my life. I had one coach in softball I didn't like very much because he was very angry. He made it feel like we were playing softball only to win, and that is why I am not playing for him, but I love, love, love being in sports.

—*Kylee, age 12*

TIPS FOR SUPPORTING ATHLETES' EMOTIONAL WELLNESS

One of the most productive steps you can take for athletes in an effort to promote emotional wellness is to demonstrate it yourself; due to the issues in sports culture, it is particularly valuable with this dimension of wellness. Athletes have much to gain when coaches express emotions and discuss difficult and happy times both on and off the court. Getting excited, showing happiness, and sharing joy with athletes and the staff is pertinent in emotional wellness. Coaches should acknowledge the mental health issues we have created in society, specifically in sports culture, and bring to light our weaknesses in supporting emotional wellness. Let athletes know you are there to help and that you will serve as a part of their support system. Show them your human side. It may be foreign to the industry, but it's healthy, and it forms a foundation for not just strong individuals, but strong athletes and teams.

In addition to modeling emotional wellness, the following are a few coaching practices that will allow you to support this important aspect of athletes' lives:

- Foster your own emotional intelligence and make time for expression of emotion so that you can better understand athletes and react with empathy.
- Throughout the season and in your routines, give players a voice.[12] You may have to help teach them how to express emotion without harming

themselves or others, but if they are never given a chance to share, they may never learn. In meetings before and after practices and games, allow for player input, keep the door open to feelings, and always express your appreciation for their sharing.

- Check in each day on coaches' and athletes' current emotional state to generate conversation and help everyone to put behaviors into perspective (for example, a coach's work-related stress may be perceived as disappointment in the team if there is no direct communication about it). This conversation can be initiated in many ways, including a quick assessment of everyone's emotional state with responses indicated by a thumbs up, down, or sideways.
- Sports can incite extremely strong emotional responses from people, so don't be surprised at the intensity of the feelings you may have to help a player express and manage.
- Embrace the spectrum of emotions that may surface when you create a safe place for athletes to feel, and remember that what athletes need emotionally from their sport will vary from day to day. They may benefit most from a physical workout to help release stress or anger. They may need the freedom associated with play to help them find calm. They may also need the connection with you and their teammates to feel supported.
- Directly discuss the value of vulnerability in sports, performance, and life to help athletes live authentically well into adulthood.
- Focus on effort and attitude or other behaviors that players can control to set the stage for developing self-efficacy and, as a result, self-esteem. Helping players through the frustrations that may be associated with performance by maintaining focus on their efforts demonstrates an emotionally healthy route to excellence.

My karate sensei was definitely one of my favorite coaches. He believed in me. He would really push us hard, but at the same time he was caring. I didn't believe in myself for a while. I didn't believe that I could fight other people off when I was doing my sparring. By the time I did get to the tournament, I got two third place medals because I fought so aggressively with the emotional strength he taught me. He was a good mentor. He helped me achieve confidence. I learned how to stand up for myself and others.

—*Gracie, age 13*

- Have fun! "Fun" is often defined by athletes as being a good sport, trying hard, experiencing positive coaching, and learning and improving.[13] When we are in the zone, not only does our performance reflect that intensity and focus, so do our emotions. We can be engulfed by personal satisfaction, joy, and laughter.
- Be cognizant of the emotions associated with injuries and the ending of sports careers.
- Recognize the role that trauma may play in a person's life. Many different coach development organizations offer research-based training in trauma-informed care and coaching practices.
- Be open to discussions about depression, anxiety, and suicide. For young people, suicide rates are as high as they have ever been.[14] Mainstream culture has created significant stigma and fear around the topic of suicide that has led to people feeling too embarrassed to reach out for help.
- Equip yourself with emergency mental health resources, such as crisis lines, that you can consult as needed. If you are coaching in a school or league, be informed of all policies and reporting procedures associated with safety concerns. Build a network of mental health professionals that you can consult when looking for referrals and advice to pass along to athletes. School-based mental health services are a great place to start.
- Specifically in relation to suicide, your role as a component of their support system is huge, but being a system of one is dangerous for both you and the athlete. A good place to start in the search for specific resources you might need is the Suicide Prevention Resource Center.[15]

Athletes trust you and may in fact feel closer to you than they do to their parents or other family members. Your relationships with players are vital in preventing the tragedy of suicide. It has been clearly documented that human connection is one of our strongest protective factors when it comes to suicide.[16] While there are many lists of warning signs to look for, the most important signal is when you notice a *change* in an athlete's behavior. Keeping in mind that suicide generally stems from a very strong desire to simply stop feeling pain, you should bring your most compassionate self to this issue and related conversations, ensuring that athletes know how to ask for help for themselves or a teammate.[17] As an influential and trusted adult in the lives of athletes, ideally you can be a person with whom they can talk about this culturally taboo subject.

APPLICATIONS IN COACH DEVELOPMENT: PROMOTING COACHES' EMOTIONAL EXPRESSION AND DEVELOPMENT OF A SUPPORT SYSTEM

While issues associated with muting our feelings have been well documented, actual progress toward change, particularly in sports, is lagging far behind our better judgment.[1] Sports' masculine roots and harmful definition of toughness leave much to be desired in terms of emotional openness, expression, and support. Complicating manners is the iconic status of coaches within the sports scene and the expectation that they are *extra* "tough." Although some coaches are on board with expressing their own feelings and embracing emotional expression by others in sports, as leaders in the system, all coaches may experience significant emotional suppression.

Efforts in coach development to support coaches' emotional wellness are essential. You may be a great sounding board for coaches, and as you develop a personal connection with them, they may begin to open up more to you about their feelings. To help them maximize their emotional wellness, you do not need to act as a therapist. Lend an ear, provide your perspective carefully, and ensure that coaches have established an emotional support system for themselves. A strong coaching staff, professional network, and/or community of practice, and healthy personal relationships may all enhance a coach's emotional wellness.[2] Both in and out of their coaching role, coaches need the safety and space to express and manage their emotions, just like anyone else.

Notes

1. Brett Rapkin, dir. *The Weight of Gold* (New York: HBO, 2020), https://www.hbo.com/documentaries/the-weight-of-gold.

2. Diane Culver and Pierre Trudel, "Clarifying the Concept of Communities of Practice in Sport," *International Journal of Sports Science & Coaching 3*, no. 1 (2008): 1–10, https://doi.org/10.1260%2F174795408784089441.

STORIES OF *WINNING WELL* IN EMOTIONAL WELLNESS

Tiffany (Ross) Anglin

Tiffany (Ross) Anglin was a standout multisport athlete. As an early child-hood education school director and high school and club volleyball coach, she has turned a traumatic sports experience into something that truly benefits others. While she faced many struggles in pursuit of her own dreams, she has become the kind of coach and leader who prioritizes others' emotional well-ness. Tiffany's compassion for the people with whom she works allows others to achieve their goals and surpass their potential, both on and off the court.

I grew up in Phoenix, Oregon, an incredibly small town, where I played sports my entire life and was well-known in the community. I was on my way to earn-ing twelve varsity letters in high school sports when, during my junior year, I signed to play softball at Villanova University. They offered me their first-ever four-year, full-ride scholarship [for softball]. It was a big deal, not just for me and my family, but for our entire community and the Villanova softball pro-gram as well. Many people who were raised in Phoenix never left town, so as soon as I signed my letter of intent to move across the country, the town was all over it. The story was on the front page of the newspaper, and news stations were contacting me for interviews. It felt good to have that recognition, but looking back, the pressure was definitely more than I could handle. I loved softball more than anything and playing at the Division I level was my dream.

While in many ways, I was on cloud nine, there were also a few red flags—there was too much pressure associated with all of this, and it felt unhealthy. My dad had been my softball coach my entire life. I was a pitcher, and whether or not it was softball season, I pitched five days a week, year-round. As a fam-ily, we didn't go on trips, we just did softball—it was life to us. When I wasn't playing on the team my dad coached, I played with a select team over four hours away from home. As we tried to fit as much softball into our days as pos-sible, I missed dances, birthday parties, and friend hangouts on a regular basis. I wasn't reluctant to do it because I loved the game more than anything, but it probably wasn't all that healthy in retrospect. Having my dad as my coach was awesome and it also came with some challenges. He was my biggest fan. He was so loving and supportive, and he pushed me to be my best. He believed in me, and together we put in the work to make my successes possible. Looking back, I don't know that I knew how to play without him, but the expectations were pretty intense.

Before leaving Phoenix for Pennsylvania, I had to let one of my most prominent high school goals slip away. I had lettered in all three sports I played from the time I was a freshman and I really wanted to end my high school career with twelve varsity letters total. My softball coach at Villanova wasn't a fan of me playing basketball my senior year. At this point, she had made me an historic offer and was setting me up with my athletic dream, so I went along with it. Not playing basketball as a senior is one of my biggest regrets, and when I look back, it's clear that even before I left, I was feeling the pressure and doing things differently than I knew I wanted and what I knew was best for me.

Arriving on campus at Villanova was an instant culture shock. For the most part, students come from very affluent families or they are there on athletic scholarships. People were wearing and talking about brand names I had never even heard of at the time. It was a hard place to make friends, and I didn't feel like I fit in. I remember telling a story in class one time about growing up in Phoenix and having everyone stare at me like I was crazy. I wasn't used to any of this. I had definitely been a big fish in a small pond back home, and here I was a total outsider. My roommate was a 6-foot-3 volleyball player who was a model from New Jersey, and we just didn't click. I can get along with pretty much anyone, but things were just so different there. I had left a boyfriend of five years back home, and I missed my family—things were hard.

The first day I showed up to softball, I vividly remember throwing the ball straight into the ground at the very beginning of warm up. It was like I had completely forgotten how to throw. At the time, I didn't know that I struggled with anxiety. I didn't even know what that was. Here I was on this beautiful field, with incredibly talented players and coaches around, experiencing my first moments in Big East conference softball, and I couldn't even play catch. Everybody knew that I was panicking, and my coach literally did nothing to help ease my nerves—if anything, she shamed me. I was just left alone by her. She had been the coach at Villanova forever, and her demeanor was just ice cold. Even though I was her first-ever athlete on a full-ride scholarship, she wouldn't give me the time of day. I was falling apart, and she just watched it happen in disgust.

As time went by, things kept going downhill. I got to a point where I could pitch in warm-up, but it wasn't like I knew I was capable of—my pitches wouldn't move. I was just off. I couldn't figure out what was happening with my body. This was just in the fall; the season hadn't even officially started. I remember we were playing Notre Dame in a preseason game and she put me on the field. I threw one bad pitch and she yanked me out of the game and didn't talk to me for weeks. This was a pattern that continued. I don't think I ever got to face more than a couple batters before I would be pulled out. I didn't know what to do; I had never really failed before. I was an all-state pitcher and player of the league prior to going to Villanova, so this was all new to me. I did not know how to deal with this, and I didn't deal with it well.

Freshman spring season (actual Big East season), I got put in a few times and I'd get yanked and never talked to. She never told me what I did wrong, what I could do differently, or what she wanted. She certainly never tried to comfort or support me in any way. At the end of my freshman year, she brought me in and because of my scholarship she couldn't let me go, so she tried to convince me to leave. I remember calling home, so upset, getting off the phone with my mom and dad, and crying my eyes out. I was devastated.

I went home that summer and remember returning to play as a sophomore at least partially just to spite my coach. Looking back, I wish I wouldn't have gone back. My sophomore year was absolutely terrible. She never put me in a game to pitch. I practiced every single day, completed all our workouts, dedicated my life to the team like you do in DI sports, and was never given a chance. Every once in a while, she would play me as a pinch runner because I was fairly fast, but I never got talked to as to why I wasn't on the field—not once. I felt trapped. It was a miserable experience, and it was clear that they owned me. I was putting in all the work, stressing out about it constantly, and my coach never did anything to help me out. I was eighteen years old and had no idea what was happening to me, but it wasn't good, and everybody knew that.

In the midst of all the emotional struggles I was facing, I had also fallen into another damaging aspect of the culture—intense dieting. The seeds were planted when I went to visit Villanova on my recruiting trip. The senior who was assigned to show me around and take me to parties was Teresa. She was one of Villanova's best players, and she had also won a competition called Body for Life. She was ripped. She had taken on this strict diet plan and was very thin and fit looking. In my offer meeting, I remember the coach telling me that I was going to be the "next Teresa," which was a big statement because she was the real deal. She was also very into the Body for Life plan, and it was clear that my coach approved of the results. There was this joke that we called ourselves the pretty team. When we would go and play other teams, their players were bigger and looked different than us. Most girls on our team were thin and "pretty"—it was clearly a recruiting thing for her, and it had a hold on the culture of our team.

When I got to campus as a freshman, our coach was definitely aware that about 60 percent of the team was doing this Body for Life thing, and, at the time, it didn't feel super, super negative. It was a twelve-week program where you eat completely clean for six days, and then, on the seventh day, you binge. There are before and after pictures. It's kind of a standard intense diet, but the impact it had on us was awful. I did this program so hardcore for twelve weeks that I dropped a lot of weight. I definitely looked different. I was ripped and I was also completing workouts with no food in my system. I'd have to do empty stomach lifting or cardio, which sounds absolutely crazy to me now. I'd go in the morning to do a workout, go to class, and then I'd go back after for softball lifting or workouts. It was nuts. The more I restricted, the more intense the binging became—that's what the diet book said we could do. We would do this as a team.

Eventually, I'd get to the point that I would binge so hard I actually felt sick, and one day I ended up throwing up. As soon as that happened, it was like a light bulb switched on in my head, and it seemed like such a good plan. I could binge as much as I wanted, and if I threw up, then none of that food would count against me. I started following that pattern most of the time when I drank alcohol. I didn't drink before going to college, so when I would drink, I would binge eat and throw up. I did that for a really long time, probably about a year. By my sophomore year, I started throwing up without drinking. It got to the point that I would throw up once a day, but I also knew that wasn't okay. So luckily, I was able to recognize that, and I started to seek help. Eventually, I was able to start minimizing the number of times I threw up in a day so that through my junior year I was still fighting the habit but stopped by my senior year.

Getting out of Villanova, out of that culture and environment was the only thing that allowed me to stop doing it. There were at least three other teammates who were purging, we had an anorexic teammate, and about half of us were on that diet program. It was an elite program—we lifted and did conditioning all year long and here we were with these terrible eating habits and negative body images. There were a lot of comments made by coaches about making sure we were in shape. In general, athletes were not supported in being true to themselves. There was a lot of secrecy in the culture and it had a lot to do with our coach. I'm not sure she knew about all of the binging and purging that was happening, but there was never any effort to prevent it in any way. Needless to say, between the disordered eating and the anxiety I was experiencing, I was a wreck. I was on the phone with my family, sobbing, every night, and I eventually made the decision to leave Villanova after my sophomore year.

I went home feeling like a complete failure. I had given up a full-ride scholarship and opportunity to play big-time college softball. It was a huge deal. My dad was devastated. I was in a very hard place, and I knew I needed to find a different plan that involved me playing college sports somewhere. I couldn't just return to Phoenix, but I was also pretty sure I couldn't get back out on the softball field. I Googled volleyball schools in DII that were nearby and contacted the coach at Seattle University to see if I could try out. I spent the summer going into my junior year training to get into volleyball shape. I didn't have access to a net or team or chances to play, so I knew it was going to be tough. I tried out and was able to walk on in fall workouts. The softball coach at Seattle U had heard about me—a transfer student who had played at Villanova—and he tried to contact me every day for about a month. There was absolutely no way that was going to happen, though; I was way too scared.

At first, the players on the volleyball team weren't very welcoming. I was super rusty and was still really battling anxiety. Every single day that I went to practice I felt that tightness in my chest and knew I wasn't playing like I could. The coach took me under her wing, however. We had tons of heart-to-heart conversations. She would give me some encouragement and positive reinforcement, and I needed that so desperately. She didn't do anything out of the ordinary, but she was kind, supportive, and communicative. It was literally life changing for me to realize how much that mattered—how much my confidence as a girl mattered. I was able to make a little speech to the team and told them a bit about my background. I explained that I just really needed to be a part of the team, and they finally gave me a chance. I didn't play much my junior year, and then I injured myself my senior year, but my life had changed drastically.

Not only was my experience with the coach night-and-day different, but the culture at Seattle U was completely different, too. Even though I had to wear spandex now as part of our uniform, I was significantly happier and was able to work through my insecurities. No one on the team really talked about bodies, eating, and dieting, so it was totally different. It wasn't a focal point, and that was incredibly helpful. Volleyball was going well, and I also made a group of friends outside of my teammates, which was very important to me. I needed that. I had my own group and I loved being with them. I was happy. My eating stuff stopped, my anxiety got a little better, and I started seeing a counselor (after going through about twelve who didn't fit, I found one who I feel like I owe my life to). The change in the culture and how I was supported by my coach totally changed my entire life.

While things ended up in a really great place and I was able to finish college feeling good about myself, there are some aspects of my experience that still remain. To this day, I still can't play sports without anxiety. Before going to Villanova, I thrived on the pressure of a game. I wanted to be the one in the spotlight with the game on the line. Even just recently, I went to play catch with my husband and I felt my whole body freeze up. I'm still too afraid to play sports. I know I can't play softball, but I can do a little volleyball, and I just know I'm nowhere near where I could be. I am constantly working through anxiety in general at this point and doing really well. When I was eighteen, I had no idea how to get help or how to even name the issue I was facing. For a long time, it was very embarrassing, and I had never felt like such a failure as I did when I left Villanova. I don't feel any shame in this anymore. I've done a ton of work around it, but it has taken me a long time. In terms of healthy eating, I feel like I do pretty well at this point, and I never would have gotten there had I not decided to change directions for myself. I eat intuitively most the time, I feel confident in my body and I have friends who are body-positive. I don't feel those pressures anymore and it is amazing. I feel very strongly about the importance of all of us sharing our stories because I know I was nowhere near the only athlete to go through all of this. We need to be talking about this more.

Everything that I learned through this experience I have taken into my own coaching. Looking back, it seems like a coach should have seen my anxiety and all that I was going through. They should have been able to help. When we're eighteen, we don't know better, and we aren't supposed to know. We need people to help guide us and get us the support we need. I feel like this is the main reason I am a good coach. I don't know everything there is to know about volleyball. I'm not super passionate about keeping up with the latest techniques, etc. I have never been that type of person or player—I never had to focus on it.

I have been successful as a coach because I really care about my players. I have never pulled a player off the court without talking to them about why—I provide all of them with that feedback. I think it's important and I want them to know that I care about them. Our relationships are incredibly valuable to me. So as a head coach, I surround myself with assistant coaches who know the game, and I focus more on the athletes and the big picture. I don't think you can be successful without the athletes feeling confident and not scared. In a way, I am grateful for everything I learned through my struggles. If I had the same experience in college as I did in high school, I may not have empathy for athletes and all that they are going through. I feel like it totally changed what I think it takes to be a strong team and really, what is important in life.

Gloria

Gloria gives her all to the youth and high school volleyball athletes she coaches. Her players feel loved and supported, not just as athletes but as people. The lessons Gloria learned and the support she received from her coaches substantially improved her emotional wellness and capacity. Their impact is what continues to drive her every day in the gym. She has been coaching for the past ten years and she doesn't take lightly her ability to pay it forward.

It doesn't feel right to tell my story regarding emotional wellness without telling a part of my family's history and where I come from. I was born to Mexican immigrant parents who came to America in 1978 with dreams that life here would provide fewer hardships. My story is my own but isn't as uncommon as one might think.

Neither of my parents are school educated. Instead of attending school, they started working for income to support their families at ages eight and nine. My dad, the product of an affair, had a traumatizing childhood. Where he comes from, the act of adultery his parents committed was the reason he was born cursed with a cleft lip. He lived his adolescent life without opportunity or treatment to have his cleft lip corrected and suffered with facial deformity and a speech impediment. As a result, he was bullied and shunned by the people who were supposed to love and care for him. He grew up alone, unwanted and without proper guidance. My whole life, and even as he stands today, I still see the pain that his childhood caused him. My mom, one of thirteen, was born to a single mother who fought every day to survive. Some of my mom's siblings did not make it to the age of five due to diseases and malnutrition. My mom was forced to work in the rivers from sunup to sundown washing the clothes of the wealthy just to be able to eat a bowl of beans at the end of the day and hope there was enough for breakfast. She was often verbally, and sometimes physically, abused at the hands of her mother. At the age of sixteen, my mom was sold to a man twice her age. Filled with rage and wonder, she gave birth to her first child at the age of eighteen. You can still see the sorrow that fills her eyes whenever she mentions her life back in Mexico.

Life is so interesting sometimes. Often, I wonder why we feel pain. Not the physical pain but the emotional pain: the kind that lasts for decades and without proper help, can eat you and everything around you, alive.

I was born in the late summer of 1987. By then, my parents had three children: ages fourteen, nine, and seven. They lived in a small two-bedroom apartment. They worked in the fields hoeing dirt and trimming bushes. It is the same job my mom retired from and the same job my dad still works today. My dad, by then, had morphed into a high-functioning, belligerent alcoholic, and my mother a depressed, angry, and lonely woman. Each of them had battles that they couldn't seem to get ahead of. It only made sense for their children to feel those effects.

Now don't get me wrong here: my parents, without a doubt, loved us all. They did the best they could with what they had. I also understand the trauma they experienced and the life they were given as children played a big part in their inability to parent the way we needed. I do not fault them for my childhood trauma or my unfortunate experiences. Had they had the ability to offer me emotional support, I know they would have.

To say that I lacked emotional support as a child is an understatement. It was, from what I can remember, nonexistent in my early years. I didn't have parents who taught me how to express my emotions in a healthy manner. I didn't have parents who told me they were proud of me. I didn't have parents who tucked me in at night. Hell, I didn't have parents who talked to me. Luckily, I had older siblings, one in particular, who cared for me. As you can imagine, there was only so much she could do for me while she was going through her own traumas. Nonetheless, she tried.

When my sister escaped our house, it was a turning point in my life. I had so much anger inside me that was covering up my emotions of sadness and sorrow. I didn't know how to express myself in a way that would be beneficial. She was my voice and my comfort. I could always depend on her. The night before she ran away, as she was packing her bags in silence and in secrecy, we wept. I was only twelve, but I knew she had to leave. I didn't have the courage to beg her to stay, and she didn't have the power to take me with her. It was a room full of hopelessness. My brother and I slept in her arms that night, and when we woke up, she was gone, and there was a new rage inside of me. That rage felt like it was stuck in the back of my throat, constantly needing to be swallowed down.

It was my sister who convinced my parents to let me play basketball. When she left, my parents tried to get me to stop playing. They claimed I had more responsibilities at home. That was true. I took on the role of taking care of my younger brother. I helped him with cooking, cleaning, laundry, homework, waking him up for school, and making sure he was completing chores so we would both stay out of trouble. It was me who would tuck him in at night and wish him sweet dreams. My parents' ways had already pushed my sister away, I couldn't allow them to take away basketball as well.

My seventh grade year of school was tough. Teachers could not understand how I could be a good student but lash out the way I did. I was often kicked out of classes and sent to timeouts for my outbursts. During basketball games, it was normal for me to foul out. If an opponent had done wrong in my eyes, I was out to get them for the rest of the game. Referees weren't exempt from that, either.

My seventh grade coaches were really the first people since my sister to support me emotionally. After an outburst of mine, they would pull me aside and talk to me. Instead of the focus of our conversation being on my outburst, often they would say, "Hey Gloria, I know you're upset. That was a questionable call. We need you to keep your head in the game. Let us get angry for you." Then, at practice or after the game, they would pull me aside and check in on me. Questions like, *How is your brother doing? How are your grades? Are you getting enough sleep? Can I help you with anything?* were common for them to ask me. They taught me calming methods to try when I was feeling angry to help keep me out of trouble and on the basketball court. I didn't know then, but they could see I was in pain. I wish that I would have let them in more than I did.

After the basketball season ended, things went downhill. I no longer had an escape, and my outbursts became more severe. The last straw for administrators at school was when I cursed out a teacher. Once I was in the dean's office, I cried. No matter how hard I tried to stop that day, I couldn't. It was all coming out. I cried for my sister; it had been months since I was allowed to see her. I cried for my parents not being able to provide me with shoes that wouldn't get me bullied. I cried for my brother who would have to witness me getting into trouble at home for what I had done. And I cried for myself. I wondered why I was given the life I was living. I was positive school administrators were going to call my parents. I can't tell you how much time had passed, but by the time the school counselor entered the room, my eyes were burning from the emptiness of tears. My stomach hurt for fear of what I had just done. I was ashamed, embarrassed, and scared.

When the counselor entered the room, she didn't yell at me or question my actions. She just let me feel. It was the first time I opened up to an adult about my home life and the trauma I had experienced. At the end of our conversation, she had signed me up to be in her anger management group for young women and weekly meetings with her. Being in anger management opened my mind and heart. Hearing the stories of my peers helped me realize that I wasn't alone. My counselor gave me tools that I lacked, and knowing that I wasn't alone helped me push myself further. I worked hard to express my feelings in a positive way.

Once basketball season started, my coaches, teammates, and even referees saw a change in me. I was able to have vulnerable conversations with my coaches about my feelings. The more love and respect I felt from them, the harder I was able to work both in the classroom and on the court.

My freshman year started new battles at home. Sports were much more demanding, with practices or games every day of the week. I loved it! My parents, not so much. They felt like time away from home was time ill spent. Every day was a battle to be allowed to do something that not only brought me joy but that I was good at. Luckily for me, I had two coaches that would advocate for me in the coming years of high school.

I didn't know that volleyball season in high school started during the summer. I had missed the opportunity to try out my freshman year. Interestingly enough, the volleyball coach kept popping up around me throughout the days at school until one day she approached me in PE class. She asked me if I would ever consider playing volleyball. Little did I know at the time, she would change my life forever.

Basketball tryout flyers started being posted around the school. I begged and pleaded with my parents to let me try out. They resisted at first but said as long as I could keep up with my chores and look after my brother, they would allow it. I built a strong relationship with my coaches right off the bat but still struggled with anger issues. There was one moment in a game that, again, was a turning point. We were playing in a predominantly white community. My coaches were African American, and my teammates were very diverse. We were a team from the inner city that didn't have a good rap sheet. Instantly, you could feel the tension in the gym. The game started off fine, but quickly you could sense that calls were being one-sided. With every unfair call, I could feel anger raising inside of me. Moments before I was about to lose it, my coach ran out onto the court. He was shouting and yelling on my behalf. I had never seen a coach that upset. All three of my coaches received technical fouls. In the middle of the chaos, I remembered what my seventh grade coach had said to me: "We need you to keep your head in the game. Let us get angry for you." I can't explain how proud I was to have them as my coaches at that moment. They had my back. I had gone my whole childhood without having one adult stand up for me or stand up for what was right. I used that fire inside of me to push my team to victory. We entered the gym as a team that day but left as a family.

I spent a lot of time in my coach's office. He helped me navigate home life, school, and becoming a young lady. He helped me recognize my strength and taught me the power of my words when expressing my emotions. By the middle of my freshman year season, I was the starting point guard for our team. I was voted most improved my freshman year, most inspirational my sophomore year, captain my junior and senior year, and most valuable player my senior year. I couldn't have done that without his constant support and trust in me to lead the team. His love, support, guidance, and encouragement pushed me to become a better teammate, player, and, most importantly, a better person.

Between my basketball and volleyball coaches, I was given tools for how to be a positive leader. My volleyball coach was always giving me articles to read, videos to watch, and even helped me with the college application process. She was the one who told me I couldn't wear jeans to a scholarship interview. She was the one who paid out of her own pocket to make sure I had the proper gear to play volleyball and who paid for me to go to volleyball summer camps. It was she who allowed my brother to come to our volleyball practices so he wouldn't be at home alone when my parents were working and I needed to practice. She was the one that hugged me when I told her I had been accepted into college. She advocated for me whenever my parents denied me the ability to do something sports or school related. She even helped me arrange details for my senior prom.

Through my coaches' emotional support, I was able to flourish as an athlete, a student, and as a person. These coaches gained my trust by being emotionally supportive. The one thing I needed most, they were able to see and provide. They went above and beyond their work duty. I worked my ass off on the court for not only myself and teammates, but for them, too. I wanted to make them proud. They saw me as more than just a player on their teams. We had built a family and I was proud to be in it.

After all of her help during high school, I was still shocked when my volleyball coach offered me an opportunity to join her coaching staff after graduation. Quite frankly, I was honored at the offer. When we hung up the phone, I cried until my eyes burned with emptiness again. This time, it wasn't because of sadness but because of joy. It was at that exact moment my purpose in life became clear. I would be able to give back every lesson that my coaches and counselor gave me. Being a coach is so much more than teaching kids proper form and formations. It is about opening your heart to young aspiring athletes and filling the role they need. Luckily for me, I had compassionate people fill the roles I needed.

Intellectual Wellness

Learning the mind is as important as understanding the body.

—*Usain Bolt*

WHAT IS INTELLECTUAL WELLNESS IN THE CONTEXT OF SPORTS?

Maximizing intellectual wellness requires dedication and effort. As we move through the world, we do what we can to build knowledge, skills, and understanding around the topics that strike at our core. We push ourselves to understand alternative perspectives, develop critical-thinking skills, and satisfy our curiosity. Expanding intellectual wellness means being open to learning and growing, and that is something we hope to maintain throughout our lives. Whether it works in our favor or not, we don't get to do anything without involving our brains, and the sports scene is no exception to that rule.

Much has been discovered about the brain in recent years specific to the learning process and the brain's connection to the body, which provides a foundation for optimizing performance. Just like we want our bodies to be in top condition, we cannot ignore the importance of a productive mindset as well. Using our understanding of the brain, purposeful planning by coaches can be aimed at maximizing learning. Structured practice and drills influence learning; however, sometimes instruction and planned activities hinder the true spirit and most permanent types of learning. With physical skills and competencies, like riding a bike, many of us were allowed to employ the most meaningful and permanent type of learning—experiential learning. We saw something and tried to emulate it. We were creative, tried a variety of approaches, and played around with what worked and what didn't. We weren't afraid of the "guess and check" method. As humans, we have a built-in sense of imagination and desire to learn and explore. Modern times and the push for increased deliberate practice have squashed our creative juices in many ways, but our brains and beings have not forgotten.[1] Learning is fun. Our brains are powerful. When applied to sport, intellectual wellness can be an exciting route to reaching our true potential.

WHY DOES INTELLECTUAL WELLNESS MATTER IN THE WORLD OF ATHLETICS?

Intellectual wellness incorporates a very different aspect of development from those addressed previously. While it crosses over with all of the dimensions of wellness, it is also independent. It is one thing to focus on physical development, for example, and the brain will automatically be involved, but it is also essential to look at the mental side of sport in isolation. Addressing intellectual wellness as a coach involves tackling topics such as mental toughness, setting the stage for lifelong learning, and supporting student-athletes in the classroom.

The mental side of sport has been studied and valued for years. We know that our mindsets have an undeniable impact on our performances and recognize the world of sports psychology as permanently relevant and ever expanding. It is said that the mental advantage in sports is where champions are separated from others.[2] A coach's mentality is extremely valuable and will certainly impact the performance of athletes. Athletes' mental game will either hinder or advance their ability to compete. Rarely, if ever, is the mental aspect of sport neutral—it has a huge impact on how we play. As you strive for excellence in yourself and the athletes you serve, we want to help you to maximize their intellectual wellness to see success in all areas of their lives.

PROBLEM: OUR BRAINS ARE GETTING IN THE WAY!

We have created a bit of a monster when it comes to fostering healthy intellectual wellness in the world of sports. Society has grown attached to the idea that there is always a right or wrong, a good or a bad. We have overemphasized winning and losing in athletics to a detrimental level.[3] Through these obsessions we have created an environment in which most of us are deathly afraid of failure. This creates a massive barrier to learning.[4] Learning requires an open mind and some level of risk-taking. If we are afraid to make a mistake, there is no way we are going to come anywhere near the "guess and check" method. As long as we are hyperfocused on the outcome of anything, we will not explore as needed to truly learn what we can.

As society grows more transactional—asking for something and getting something immediately in return—people have become bored with processes. Athletics are not alone in suffering through this dilemma, but within sports we have wonderful opportunities to counter this tendency. Doing the work is not always glamorous, but it is necessary and rewarding, especially for individuals who want to be their best. As sports follow cultural trends, it's too easy to sit back, point a finger of blame at someone else, play the victim, and settle for mediocrity. We know that coaches and athletes can do better. We know that a growth mindset is one of the keys to success, and we can foster that in ourselves and our players en route to achieving greatness.[5]

Table 4.1. Characteristic Beliefs and Behaviors Associated with a Fixed or Growth Mindset Linked to Key Concepts in Learning and Development in Sport and Physical Activity

Beliefs and Behaviors Associated with a Growth Mindset	Key Concepts in Learning and Development	Beliefs and Behaviors Associated with a Fixed Mindset
With effort, good strategies, and help, people can change and develop most qualities and abilities		*People's qualities and abilities are largely predetermined, inherited, and/or unchangeable once developed*
Doing one's best, trying hard Learning and improving Many types of success	Success	Establishing superiority with least effort Being gifted or a natural Success as winning
See the bigger picture Be patient, see progress in steps Use self-referenced goals	Motivation	Want immediate results Seek quick fixes Compare self to others
Relish challenge Seek hard but realistic tasks	Challenges	Avoid challenge if risky Seek easier or unrealistic tasks

(continued)

Table 4.1. *Continued*

Beliefs and Behaviors Associated with a Growth Mindset *With effort, good strategies, and help, people can change and develop most qualities and abilities*	Key Concepts in Learning and Development	Beliefs and Behaviors Associated with a Fixed Mindset *People's qualities and abilities are largely predetermined, inherited, and/or unchangeable once developed*
See effort as investment—effort essential for learning and achievement	Effort	Not cool to show effort—effort needed by those struggling to achieve
Persist and find new ways Engage in problem-solving	Obstacles	Demotivated, lose focus May feel or act helpless
View criticism as valuable feedback	Criticism	Ignore, dispute, or denigrate criticism
Informative—a wake-up call Stimulates constructive reflection Can be motivating	Failure	Threat to self-esteem and identity Prolonged anger, despair, blame May lead to withdrawal
Draw inspiration and ideas from others' success	Success of Others	Feel threatened or demoralized by the success of others
Regain composure and rebound from setbacks Can maintain robustness during uncertain periods	Resilience	Struggle to retain composure and rebound from setbacks Struggle to maintain robustness during tough times
Actively ask for advice/help Look to build network, gain insights and learn from others	Support Seeking	Uncomfortable asking for help May remain isolated or hide uncertainty/confusion
More open to experience/new ideas because of beliefs that people can change and find learning and insights from many situations	Openness to Experience	Less inclined to be open to experience/new ideas because one's predetermined capacities have dictated what can be learned and how

Source: Abbe Brady and Samantha Hughes, 2013, cited in Abbe Brady and Bridget Grenville-Cleave, *Positive Psychology in Sport and Physical Activity: An Introduction* (New York: Routledge, 2018), 109.

Finally, when highlighting issues related to intellectual wellness, in the hypercompetitive sports environment, the idea of the student-athlete is often undervalued. A small percentage of athletes break through the amateur boundary, so supporting education and career preparation must not fall to the wayside.

A NOTE ON FEASIBILITY AS IT RELATES TO INTELLECTUAL WELLNESS

In relation to maximizing intellectual wellness, a few barriers that you may encounter include, but are not limited to, the following:

- Intellectual abilities and maturity, even among athletes of the same age, can be vastly different from one athlete to the next.
- Mindsets are very ingrained in most of us, and while they can be shifted, it is not likely to happen overnight. There may be a very good (and protective) reason that someone behaves as they do, especially in relation to failure.
- When basic needs are not met, intellectual wellness will take a back seat. This will happen in relation to mental acuity in sports as well as in school.
- We all have a limited capacity to function at a high level intellectually within a day, which includes the mental demands of sports.
- Athletes' learning styles and preferences vary.
- Athletes may not have access to the tools needed to study the game outside of practice, and their environment may or may not support such work.

While this list is not exhaustive, taking the time to acknowledge potential barriers to wellness is imperative.

Intellectual wellness in sports promotes lifelong learning, a growth mindset, creative abilities, and critical thinking skills both in and out of sport; prioritizes educational and career endeavors; and fosters the development of the mental side of sport.

WHERE ARE YOU NOW?
1. How do you feel about your current intellectual wellness?
2. How do you feel about the intellectual wellness of the athletes you coach?
3. How much of a priority is it for you to support your athletes' intellectual wellness?
4. How well-informed and prepared do you feel to help maximize intellectual wellness in the athletes you coach?
5. How do your personal and coaching practices support or detract from your athletes' intellectual wellness?

TIPS FOR SUPPORTING YOUR OWN INTELLECTUAL WELLNESS
The following are a variety of tips for maximizing your personal intellectual wellness that can also be applied with others to support their intellectual wellness:

- Embrace a spirit of curiosity and engage in lifelong learning. This can include listening to motivating podcasts, reading books, talking to others, and attending conferences. It can be formal or informal. Most importantly, remain open to possibilities and absorb as much as you can from others. Let learning happen and welcome it with excitement.
- Try something new. Take a class. Remember what it is like to learn, and use that experience to relate to athletes.
- While you are giving your best effort as a coach (as well as in other aspects of life), expect to make mistakes. When we truly push ourselves to be our best, we have to take chances and it will not always be perfect. Embrace that imperfection and any mistakes as opportunities to learn and improve.
- Reflect on your coaching practice and get accustomed to constantly evolving as a professional.[6]
- Put all of your effort into striving for excellence and embrace the process. Focus entirely on the current moment and allow yourself to be excited or determined, whichever fits the moment best.
- Visualize success. Use as many of your senses as possible (typically, the more senses involved in visualization, the more powerful the effects) and imagine yourself overcoming a variety of coaching challenges.
- Acknowledge your strengths and weaknesses as a coach and give them both attention. You will want to maximize your strengths and take the time to

seek out advice and/or ideas in the areas in which you feel deficient. Having this humility will serve a key role in helping you to be the best coach you can be.

TIPS FOR SUPPORTING ATHLETES' INTELLECTUAL WELLNESS

In addition to the ideas listed above that can be used by anyone, the following are a few pointers centered on the promotion of intellectual wellness in others:

- Model, model, model. Let athletes know that you are continuing to grow and learn by admitting your faults, taking chances, and showing enthusiasm for progress. Truly embrace processes over outcomes in yourself and athletes.
- Use the process of transfer to maximize capacity. Knowledge, skills, and abilities can be transferred from one sport to another, or they may be transferred to or from something outside of sports. The more connections you help an athlete to make with something they are learning, the stronger that learning tends to be.
- Build a safe environment in which mistakes are valued as opportunities for growth. Let players know that, as people, they are more important than their performances.

My favorite coach is Marcus. He's really good at making you do easy stuff first and then working up to the real thing. He doesn't try to teach you just super fancy moves first. He tries to let you understand how to play. If I mess up, he's always like, "So close! Try again, I bet you'll make it!" So, he's really encouraging, and I think he's super nice too. He challenges me the right amount. He's the best coach I've ever had, and he makes it really fun.

—*Chase, age 7*

- Prioritize effort over anything else when it comes to performance. If you can get athletes to give their all, the sky's the limit.
- Challenge athletes appropriately (employing the zone of proximal development)[7] and help them strive for the mental state of flow.[8] Do what you can to help athletes operate in those ideal learning states.

- Help athletes to stay focused on the current play or moment in competitions and practices. Holding on to successes and/or failures that have passed adds unnecessary internal dialogue that takes an athlete's attention away from what matters most—the here and now. Beating ourselves up over the last play or wishing we were performing like we did the night before impedes our mental ability to give our best. The most successful athletes find a way to constantly strive for excellence within every moment. This level of focus may take a lot of practice (and be difficult to maintain), but it is required to maximize potential.

- Help athletes to find their "why" and, in the process, prioritize behaviors for long-term development.[9] If athletes are clear on their purpose for investing time and effort into their sport, outcomes or short-term results become less meaningful, and they can truly strive for their potential with vigor.

- Use clear, specific, positively stated feedback to help athletes learn and improve. When they know exactly what it is you are encouraging them to do and they feel supported, they can then—and only then—engage in the learning process.

- Reflection for players is as important as it is for you as a coach. Taking the time to address how things went after each game or practice session is essential for solidifying learning. When you discuss performance with players (and better yet, when you get their input and involvement in the discussion), you have the opportunity to purposefully plan your next action steps, and you can help them to internalize the value of practice. Throughout the season, you should consistently plan your activities, implement them, and evaluate them, then make adjustments accordingly. A thorough reflection involves taking the time to discuss what went well, what you might be able to do better, and what you want to focus on next time.[10] This should be a standard daily routine.

- Invest time in teaching the mental side of the game. Help players to *understand* strategies and tactics as opposed to just throwing them into a play. Lead them in becoming "students of the game"; don't just expect it to come at a certain age or level of commitment. This allows them to continue on in sports indefinitely and can serve as a great way to build confidence in learning in general.

- Remember that the individual statistics you track and discuss with athletes and the film clips you watch may impact players' confidence. While you may have something to show them that can maximize their learning, keep in mind there are people behind those stats and those clips.
- Many coaches rely heavily on game and/or practice film as a teaching tool. Recognize the level of critical thinking and the depth of strategic knowledge that is required to use a film session well. Depending upon the level at which you coach, time spent watching film may be better employed elsewhere. If nothing else, you may need to invest significant effort in teaching players what to look for and how to use that information. Some players are looking just for their own mistakes or highlight reel moments along with those of their teammates.
- Remember that athletes have a limited attention span dependent upon their mental maturity, investment in the sport, and being matched with an intellectual challenge level that does not overwhelm or bore them. Three-hour-long practice sessions, for example, may be ineffective for many athletes—both mentally and physically.
- Keep in mind all of the intellectual demands placed on an athlete throughout the day. You may need to adjust your expectations of athletes' abilities to study their sport after a long day of thinking and engaging at a high level in school.
- Build a culture that supports academic growth and the concept of the student-athlete. Support and reinforce academic standards and celebrate academic victories for all players according to their unique academic goals. This also applies to life and career aspirations and successes. Regardless of the level at which you coach, there will always be other valuable aspects of life outside of sports to recognize and support.
- Teach and encourage visualization. Help players to use their minds to get over their fears and through their biggest barriers. They may need to be able to do it in their own minds to even stand a chance of doing it on the court.

APPLICATIONS IN COACH DEVELOPMENT: PROMOTING A GROWTH MINDSET AND REFLECTION THROUGH A COACH-CENTERED APPROACH

As explained by Dieffenbach, "Across all levels of sport, the responsibility for the best possible outcomes has always been placed on the shoulders of the coach."[1] As a result, coaches may feel an undue level of accountability or an undeserved amount of credit for a performance, holding themselves more responsible for the actions of others than is reasonable. In terms of helping coaches to employ growth mindset concepts in their own development, this aspect of sport culture challenges progress. As coaches strive for excellence, perfectionism provides a substantial barrier to intellectual wellness and learning, and may prove challenging for coach developers. Guiding coaches to employ a productive mindset has the potential to pay off exponentially.

Establishing a coach-centered climate that is characterized by authenticity, personal support and connection, and appreciation for effort and failure and is centered on long-term growth will help to ensure that coaches are able to fully engage as learners.[2] You may be able to leverage coaches' competitive nature and knowledge of the science of learning to help them focus on their essential role as a learner. In the process of emphasizing continuous growth, being particularly sensitive to the pressures of coaching will help you to create a learning environment that functions effectively within the high-stakes field of sports leadership.

One of the hallmark characteristics of a strong coach development plan is its individualized nature.[3] Considering the context along with individual competencies and aspirations to formulate a personalized, long-term coach development plan should be at the heart of your work.

In addition to theories for teaching adults, coach developers are most effective when they keep in mind practices that apply to *all* learners to maximize coaches' learning while simultaneously helping coaches to address athletes' intellectual wellness. As you establish a strong learning environment, don't hesitate to look to education for potential keys to success. As Crisfield explains, "Coaching and coach development may also be closely aligned functionally to the well-established teaching profession, not simply due to their focus on skill acquisition but also to their aspiration to contribute to the development of the whole person rather than simply the athlete."[4]

The International Sport Coaching Framework indicates three types of knowledge that are required for successful coaching.[5] In addition to prioritizing professional knowledge and interpersonal knowledge (to which very few practitioners would contend), the framework includes intrapersonal knowledge as an equally valuable component in a coach's toolkit. To consistently strive for better, we must consistently observe and reflect on our practice.[6] While some coaches regularly observe and reflect upon athlete or team performances, it is much less common for them to engage in reflection on their own coaching. Shifting or broadening their perspective to set coaching process goals will help coaches to embrace the concept of their own development and sets the stage for meaningful conversations with you. Be prepared to help them work through the cultural emphasis on athlete and team outcomes and guide them to isolate their coaching practices as a point of examination.

If the goal is long-term coaching success, coaches themselves must see the value in continual development as they move beyond traditional, episodic coach education.[7] To personalize the learning experience and growth for each coach, self-reflection by coaches may be one of the most influential learning activities a coach developer supports.[8] Using a variety of formats—including journaling, self-assessments, discussion, video analysis, and more—coaches are able to dive into what they coach as well as how they coach. It is the former that may have the greatest potential impact on their performance and also may be where they are lacking intention.

There are a variety of effective reflection strategies and techniques from which to choose. One method that is supported by the International Council for Coaching Excellence uses the acronym GRIP (goals, reflect, input, plan).[9] This process can be completed by the coach themselves or with your support as follows:

1. Upon completion of a practice session or game, the first step is to ask what the coach's *goals* were. In this phase, it is important to push coaches to not just identify an outcome goal for athletes, but to include a process goal for their coaching as well.

2. In the *reflection* phase, guide coaches in evaluating what went well, what could be better, what they would do next time, and what success looks like.[10]

3. After self-reflection, have coaches seek *input* on the same aspects that they have evaluated. Again, there are many different sources to consider for this insight, one of them being your feedback as the coach developer. You may need to help them decide who else to involve in their reflection process, when, how, and to what extent.

4. Finally, help coaches to *plan* for their improvement. Focusing on just one piece of information that surfaced through reflection may help to

prioritize an area with the greatest potential for learning and can make the development process more powerful and manageable for coaches.

Ultimately, the goal is to make reflection second nature for coaches as they consistently repeat the GRIP process, with and without your participation.

Notes

1. Kristen Dieffenbach, "Frameworks for Coach Education and Development," in *Coach Education Essentials: Your Guide to Developing Sport Coaches,* edited by Kristen Dieffenbach and Melissa Thompson (Champaign, IL: Human Kinetics, 2020), 7.

2. Harley Ellenberger (@harleyberger), "The ELM Tree of Mastery Image," Twitter, March 22, 2017, https://twitter.com/HarleyBerger/status/844706286633717760; International Council for Coaching Excellence, "Facilitation Handbook: Introduction to Facilitation Skills," presented at the 2018 ICCE/USCCE Coach Developer Academy, Orlando, FL, 2018; Abbe Brady and S. Hughes, "Exploring the Impact of a Best Future-Self Intervention on the Well-Being of Early Career Sport Coaches: The Mediating Role of Mindset," presented at the 3rd Biennial Meeting of the British Psychological Society's Division of Sport and Exercise Psychology, Manchester, England, December 2013; Carol Dweck, *Mindsets* (New York: Ballantine Books, 2006).

3. Kathryn L. Russell, "Differentiated Instruction through Engaged Lecturing for Coach Development," on *Coach Education and Development in Sport: Instructional Strategies,* edited by Bettina Callary and Brian Gearity (New York: Routledge, 2020), 190–200; Carol Ann Tomlinson and Jay McTighe, *Integrating Differentiated Instruction & Understanding by Design: Connecting Content and Kids* (Alexandria, VA: Association for Supervision and Curriculum Development, 2006).

4. Penny Crisfield, "Long-Term Coach Development Process." In *Coach Education Essentials: Your Guide to Developing Sport Coaches,* edited by Kristen Dieffenbach and Melissa Thompson, 281. Champaign, IL: Human Kinetics, 2020.

5. International Council for Coaching Excellence and Association of Summer Olympic International Federations, International Sport Coaching Framework: Version 1.1, 2012. https://www.icce.ws/_assets/files/news/ISCF_1_aug_2012.pdf.

6. International Council for Coaching Excellence, "Facilitation Handbook: Introduction to Facilitation Skills." Presented at the 2018 ICCE/USCCE Coach Developer Academy, Orlando, FL, 2018.

7. Crisfield, "Long-Term Coach Development Process"; Sergio Lara-Bercial and John Bales, "International Coach Education and Development: A Case Study." In *Coach Education Essentials: Your Guide to Developing Sport Coaches,* edited by Kristen Dieffenbach and Melissa Thompson, 209–36. Champaign, IL: Human Kinetics, 2020.

8. Mark Bisson, *Coach Yourself First: A Coach's Guide to Self-Reflection* (Market Harborough, UK: Troubadour, 2017); James M. Kouzes and Barry Z. Posner, "Leadership Begins with an Inner Journey," *Leader to Leader* 60 (2011): 22–27. https://doi.org/10.1002/ltl.464.

9. International Council for Coaching Excellence and Association of Summer Olympic International Federations, International Sport Coaching Framework: Version 1.1.

10. Sarah McQuade, "How to Learn as a Coach from Self-Reflection." USA Football Blogs (blog), December 29, 2017. https://blogs.usafootball.com/blog/5257/how-to-learn-as-a-coach-from-self-reflection.

STORIES OF *WINNING WELL* IN INTELLECTUAL WELLNESS

Laurie Milligan

Laurie Milligan played basketball at the University of Tennessee and credits Coach Pat Summitt with helping her to develop mental toughness. The lessons she learned as a Lady Vol have impacted both her personal and professional life and continue to lead to great success. Laurie was a champion on the court and is carrying her coach's legacy of the Definite Dozen[11] forward to maximize intellectual wellness in herself and others.

Growing up, I always had a ball in my hand or on my foot. Soccer was my first love, but basketball was close behind. I felt a draw toward the competition, the skill it took to achieve the outcome. It was something I could place my focus on and do it well. We played anything and everything from hide and go seek, to H-O-R-S-E, to building forts, riding bikes, and pretending we were adults making our way in life. I didn't have helicopter parents watching over every move I made or every argument I had with a friend. We had to figure out how to get along. My parents weren't fighting my battles or rescuing me from my mistakes. This formed the foundation for my mental toughness, and I'm very grateful for it.

There was not a lot of room for self-pity growing up, and according to my coaches, making excuses was a form of whining or complaining. I believe my coaches helped prepare me, as best as I could be, for the extreme Division I college athletic experience and being coached by the late Pat Summitt.

As early as twelve years old, I started receiving recruiting letters. I had a lot of options, but I knew playing basketball for Pat at the University of Tennessee was going to be hard-core and that it would benefit me and my life forever. The choice I made to play for Pat was the best decision because she didn't promise me a starting position or playing time. This was a high-level program, and I would have to earn it.

Pat pushed me with respect and consistency, reinforcing my resilience and work ethic. She also taught me how to perceive all situations in a positive way. The consistency Pat portrayed regarding how to respond to adversity was powerful and it has stuck with me in my adult life.

My freshman year we lost the national championship to UCONN. Pat took us to the locker room afterward and said, "Feel what you are feeling right now. Feel the loss—the weight of the disappointment—but tomorrow we are back to work." Then my sophomore year we won the national championship, and it was awesome; our feelings as a team were through the roof. Pat took us to the locker room and said, "Enjoy what you are feeling right now. Celebrate it, but tomorrow morning we are back to work." She treated failure like she treated success.

Everything about Pat's coaching was centered around mental toughness. She would ask me where my mental game was each day. That was her biggest point of emphasis as a coach. She really got in my face as a point guard. She would say to me, "Your team's success depends on you and how you are carrying yourself. If you are erratic, your team is going to be erratic. If you are calm, steady, strong, and confident, then your team is going to follow suit." Mental toughness was a huge thing for Pat, and I think it really helped shape how I deal with my emotions. Her approach was consistent—rarely satisfied and with a bigger goal in mind.

I had two goals when I was at Tennessee in addition to winning a national championship: I wanted to graduate with a 3.0 GPA or higher and secure a job. I wanted to set myself up for success and give myself options in life as best I could. This was another way mental toughness was taking root in my life after college. I started working in basketball promotions at Adidas America. When I started, I remember seeking constant feedback from my boss. I was used to that kind of feedback from Pat, pushing me to get better or critiquing the last play. I had to come to terms with feedback in the professional world. It was one of the toughest transitions for me after college basketball. I had to find the motivation inside of me: my own kind of Pat.

I find I grow best if I push through tough circumstances while learning from them. It is important to keep going—developing the skills so you can get back up whenever you fall. Going through marriage, divorce, and having my daughter has really shown me my growth mindset matters. I went through some very low times after my divorce. The process left me emotionally and financially devastated. I knew in the back of my mind, "Tomorrow morning, I have to get up and get to work." I felt the Pat Summitt Nudge: "Whether you've failed, or you've prevailed, you get up the next morning and get to work." Being pushed beyond my ability by Pat built this muscle mentally inside of me.

Because of how I have progressed with mental toughness, I feel more in order. I feel like I am the toughest I have ever been. Working in the real estate industry has allowed me to use all of Pat's principles. It is based on self-motivation, mental toughness, and self-discipline. Being coached by Pat really formed the way I view situations. I learned to limit my excuses and to value commitment. The guidance of Pat and the Definite Dozen have transformed my professional life and led me to become the CEO of my own company. Pat knew we were going on to be doctors, politicians, entrepreneurs, and influencers of the next generation. She knew she was developing women who would change the world. Those who contribute positively. Those who know how to reflect on their emotions and use them effectively. Those who seek solutions rather than complain. Those that push through the hard muck and are an example to the lives around them.

I have been given the opportunity to train and coach kids since graduating college, and every day I hear Pat's words coming out of me. I remain passionate about what I was taught, those things that have helped make me a stronger woman. I continue to use Pat's Definite Dozen to increase self-esteem and empower athletes to work hard in every aspect of their lives. We can't choose our hardships, but we can choose how we respond to them.

Cara Cocchiarella

As someone who loves to learn on a daily basis, Cara Cocchiarella attributes much of her mindset and appreciation for growth to her sports experience. Her coaches taught her to consistently strive for excellence, and she does her part to pass that intellectual wellness on to others with whom she works. While Cara consistently builds athletes' capacity to thrive in life through athletics, she never knew how much her own life would desperately lean on the mental toughness she developed in sports.

Organized sports were a big part of my childhood, though the games we played in the backyard, races we held in the street, and competitions we created on the monkey bars were probably even more formative. My brother and I, along with the neighborhood kids, would make up games, work together, keep score, and compete. Acting as a "poor sport" was one of the biggest violations we could possibly commit, so from a young age I learned to play as hard as I could, and to win and lose with grace and empathy.

I experienced quite a bit of success as a high school athlete, playing all three seasons, and practicing and competing as much as possible in the summers (as long as I could still fit in time at the lake). I played basketball, volleyball, track and field, and Little League softball until I was too old to play anymore. In college, I walked on and played one season for the University of Montana basketball team. Throughout my athletic career, most of my coaches believed in me and cared about me as a person. The connections I built with those coaches served an essential role in me striving for excellence, both on and off the court. With their help I learned to push myself and discovered that my actual limits were well beyond what I may have originally thought. They reconfirmed what I had learned in the back yard—that I could give my best, and win or lose, I could always learn and come back stronger. My coaches showed me how enjoyable it was to work hard and improve. Through significant efforts, they taught me how to focus and move beyond the last play in order to be my best for the next moment. They supported my love for working on a team and my passion for the game itself. I learned that there is never a reason to give up—on myself or others. My coaches taught me to see the potential in any situation and to pursue it with all my heart.

Those coaches, who served as role models to me, became some of my biggest fans as I jumped into the coaching world with both feet. I emulated many of the practices I had learned from my best coaches and exerted considerable effort building my coaching skills. Over time, I established a strong philosophy, and I continued to grow from one season to the next, learning from every athlete I coached. The more time I spent reiterating with athletes the lessons I learned in my playing days, the more those lessons seemed to shape my identity as a person. As the teams I coached gathered trophies and accolades, it grew increasingly clear that the impact of sports goes well beyond the court. I always knew that the people in sports were a priority to me, but what I didn't know was that sports, and the mindset I developed as an athlete and a coach, would one day save my life.

In December 2018, during my traditional Friday workout, things didn't feel right. From the moment I started to warm up, I felt like I couldn't catch my breath. Within the next four days, I visited an urgent care facility twice and discovered a tumor bigger than a softball sitting in my chest cavity, right on top of my heart.

The next couple of weeks would be the most difficult weeks of my life up to this point. It was extremely difficult to get any testing done or to schedule with any doctors due to the holidays and holiday breaks. In the meantime, breathing was growing increasingly difficult. As the tumor grew, fluid continued accumulating in my lungs, and my heart was being increasingly compressed. Just getting enough oxygen to my cells in order for me to move around was a challenge. I couldn't eat much because there was no room in my abdomen for food. I couldn't lay down to sleep because the pressure of the tumor would completely block my ability to breathe. I got to the point that I could only take a few steps at a time without needing to stop, catch my breath, and regain the strength needed to take a few more. It was terrifying.

Just after New Year's, I found myself in the intensive care unit, in desperate need of help. I had been diagnosed with a rare form of lymphoma that would require immediate and intense treatment. Simultaneously, I needed significant help in order to be able to breathe again. I went through numerous medical procedures, was intubated on a ventilator, and started what doctors described as "very intense" chemotherapy. I was able to leave the hospital after some time, but for the next eight months, treatment was excruciating. The list of side effects I experienced is difficult to fathom to this day, and I know things could still be worse. There were many days that I felt like I could barely function and others that seemed somewhat manageable, but there was always a struggle to some degree. I gave my best effort every day and I learned to accept help from others. My family and friends provided me with unbelievable support, and my medical care team was absolutely fantastic.

While I have made considerable progress, I still have a long way to go, and it is likely that I may not return completely to where I was physically before all of this. Most importantly, I'm still here. There was a time when I did not think that was an option. The treatment is working, I have learned an immeasurable amount about myself, others, and cancer, and I am a better and stronger friend, family member, partner, and woman than I was before. I would never wish this upon myself (and certainly not anyone else) in a million years, but this fight has helped me to grow in ways that I never expected. Being able to connect all of this to the lessons I learned in sports has helped me to make sense of things that have otherwise been virtually impossible to explain.

As an athlete and a coach, I loved a challenge. If things were too easy, I knew I wasn't getting any better. I liked to win just as much, if not more, than the next competitor, but I thrived in the sports environment because to me it was about doing my absolute best. I had coaches who emphasized this perspective, and it has helped me to achieve many things in life. With their influence and my consistent practice and effort, I built a very strong growth mindset. It was essential to my success in sports, but I never expected to have to lean on it to survive. Cancer isn't pretty. It has and continues to challenge me constantly and in ways I never anticipated. Because I learned through sports how to recognize struggles as opportunities for growth, I have grown stronger in every aspect of my life. There have been many days in which I may have lost a battle here and there, but that isn't enough to get me down. Just like I did on the court, track, or field as an athlete and as I encouraged all of the athletes I coached to do, I continue on now in this battle because I can.

In addition to a growth mindset that has allowed me to truly give my all, I have also developed a mindful approach to life that strongly resonates with my experience as an athlete. In order to be successful in sports, I learned to be

100 percent present in the moment. My most challenging athletic endeavors required my full attention and engagement. As I have discovered, a battle with cancer is not so different from a battle with any opponent in this regard. It has demanded my focus and commitment at a shocking level. While I am confident that I and many others will ultimately triumph, I am not sure that it is possible at all times to beat cancer, even if we survive it. Some days, it gets the best of me. If I try to deny the times I feel miserable, however, I would be setting myself up for failure. Being honest about how I feel has been both difficult and empowering. Just like athletic challenges demanded my entire focus and all of my energy at different times, I have been able to bring that same intensity to the fight for my life, and I am fortunate to have had years of practice as an athlete and a coach.

Finally, through all of the different sporting experiences I have had in my life, no matter how crushing the blow or defeat, I have learned to get back up. Much to my dismay as a young athlete, I learned over time that losing truly is part of playing the game. As I have taken on increasingly difficult activities or strong opponents, I have discovered that I can always bounce back. With cancer, this ability in me has been tested to the max. There have been many times that sickness, treatment, or some of the side effects have gotten the best of me. There have been days when I've been knocked down literally thousands of times and even moments in which it seems I've experienced multiple setbacks. What I know—and one of the main lessons I have learned from sports for which I am incredibly grateful—is that I can get back up. That saying about the champion being the one who gets up one more time than others rings true for me. It may not look pretty, but that doesn't matter. With the help of the best team I could have ever imagined (my medical team along with my family and friends), I will be the champion here, and I will continue to get back up.

I have mental training from sports to credit for a significant portion of this victory. Sure, some of this I learned outside of the sports arena, but the aforementioned lessons were reinforced in a powerful setting for me throughout my life. As I look back at my career as an athlete and a coach, the most valuable impact my coaches had on me had nothing to do with Xs and Os and everything to do with consistently striving to reach my potential on all fronts. The efforts of those coaches who invested in my intellectual wellness have proved successful in the ultimate battle. They taught me how to mentally survive a challenge, and I don't know that I will ever be able to sufficiently express my gratitude for how that has all played out.

5

Spiritual Wellness

Champions aren't made in gyms. Champions are made from something they have deep inside them—a desire, a dream, a vision.

—*Muhammad Ali*

WHAT IS SPIRITUAL WELLNESS IN THE CONTEXT OF SPORTS?

For coaches accustomed to reading coaching books filled with Xs and Os, the emergence of spirituality in a coaching book may be surprising. Spiritual wellness in athletics goes beyond traditional thinking of spirituality to also include morals and personal philosophies. In terms of embracing the holistic nature of wellness in yourself and athletes, spirituality is a key component, which research indicates is essential in striving for athletic excellence.[1]

Spiritual wellness comes in countless forms. Whether you practice a specific religion or not, hopefully you have identified what matters most to you and have decided on guiding principles that inspire your behaviors. When someone is living out spiritual wellness, they demonstrate actions aligned with priorities and employ ethical decision-making. In the world of athletics, we encounter ethical dilemmas on a regular basis (for example, actions associated with a winning-at-all-costs mentality). For some people, spirituality may involve a higher power. For all of us, it includes identifying our motivation, applying core values, and making the most of our opportunities. Core values help you to exemplify what you want your program to be most known for (for example, hard work or positive attitudes). They are a guide in times of crisis and a foundation of your daily work.

WHY DOES SPIRITUAL WELLNESS MATTER IN THE WORLD OF ATHLETICS?

In every walk of life, we are faced with a plethora of choices every day. The decisions we make should align with our values and reinforce our priorities. When our actions and values are competing, our spiritual wellness is deprived. In the midst of bringing out the best that we can in ourselves and others in a season, the last thing we need is to be in a constant moral crisis.

The sports scene is intense. Emotions are flying, people are testing their own limits as well as the limits of others, and relationships are plentiful and include different power dynamics and social expectations. There is a *lot* going on. As a coach and/or athlete, one of the most important things you can do to equip yourself for that intensity is to determine what matters most to you.

As a new coach, there's a good chance that someone told you to develop your coaching philosophy before you did anything else. We know from all sectors of society that strong leadership involves clearly establishing core values and building the systems that support those values.[2] Sports are not immune to this need and may demand a clearer identity than the average environment. When we are giving our best effort, pushing ourselves to the max and asking others to jump on board with us, our vision and mission should be crystal clear. Specific to sports, the addition of competition brings a whole new level of complexity, putting at risk our commitment to be true to ourselves and maximize wellness for all.

One of the most notable characteristics of coaching (that gives it that complex nature) is the fact that some parts of coaching can be planned, but much of it must be improvised. The clearer our philosophy and the better we know ourselves, the more likely we are to respond and react to things appropriately—within our value system—in the heat of the moment.

When faced with ethical challenges, players should be able to easily predict coaches' expectations, reactions, and choices. This consistency exists when a coach brings spiritual wellness into a program. It doesn't mean that everything will be perfect, and as long as people are not causing harm in any way, there is not necessarily a right or wrong approach. Moral dilemmas, while challenging, may lead to further development of your philosophy. As you learn, grow, and change as a coach and a person, your values will be adjusted accordingly.

When we compete for something bigger than ourselves and the momentary glory of victory, the potential for sustained success skyrockets. As a coach, if your actions clearly demonstrate your philosophy and values at work, you will have spiritual wellness propelling you to the top of your game in a respectable manner. In a similar vein, it is the conviction of athletes (regardless of the source of that conviction) that allows them to see their best in performance as well. Both athletes and coaches will be challenged with ethical dilemmas, and our responses improve with conscious reflection, discussion, and practice. We all have the opportunity to push our experience to the next level when we are committed to a purpose and are grounded in a strong moral foundation.[3]

PROBLEM: WE FORGOT WHY WE CAME HERE IN THE FIRST PLACE!

Sports have somehow become void of humanity; the priorities are off. An excessive amount of energy and focus is put into the score at the end of the game or match, diminishing the value and purpose of sports. The development and nourishment of conviction to compete is much more powerful than any box score will ever be.

Coaching is a multifaceted, complex profession, so it can be easy to get lost in all of its different dynamics, but it is not too much to ask coaches why they do what they do and expect them to consistently have an answer. There are a million ways to coach athletes and probably a million *great* ways, at that. Employing spiritual wellness in coaching is not about choosing the right way; it's about choosing the route aligned with your values and acting in a manner consistent with your identity.

Your coaching philosophy should be visible in practically everything you do; however, it takes concerted effort. Identifying your values and wholeheartedly embracing them requires courage. When there is an easy solution that violates your core values, doing the right thing takes conviction.

A NOTE ON FEASIBILITY AS IT RELATES TO SPIRITUAL WELLNESS

In relation to maximizing spiritual wellness, a few barriers that you may encounter include, but are not limited to, the following:

- There are a variety of potential conflicts of interest that may arise between traditional sports activities and various spiritual practices (e.g., spring sports tournaments coinciding with Ramadan).

- Standard scheduling of sports activities may or may not support all spiritual practices.
- Uniforms and expected dress codes may interfere with spiritual traditions.
- Spiritual wellness is a lifelong journey in which we all develop at different rates.

While this list is not exhaustive, taking the time to acknowledge potential barriers to wellness is imperative.

Spiritual wellness in sports promotes each individual's sense of purpose and meaning in life and in sports (can be religious or not), reinforces ethical decision-making and core values within a program, and embraces the unique perspectives, experiences, and values of all athletes.

WHERE ARE YOU NOW?
1. How do you feel about your current spiritual wellness?
2. How do you feel about the spiritual wellness of the athletes you coach?
3. How much of a priority is it for you to support your athletes' spiritual wellness?
4. How well-informed and prepared do you feel to help maximize spiritual wellness in the athletes you coach?
5. How do your personal and coaching practices support or detract from your athletes' spiritual wellness?

TIPS FOR SUPPORTING YOUR OWN SPIRITUAL WELLNESS
The following is a short list of considerations for you as you build your spiritual wellness as a coach:

- Identify your personal core values and demonstrate them regularly in your actions. There may be values that you espouse specific to athletics, but ensuring you have a clear moral base for yourself will help you to determine what matters most in sports.

- Determine the core values that you want to employ as a coach and consistently discuss them with your coaching staff and athletes. Limit your selection to two to four focal points so that athletes can truly embrace them. Choose values that can be applied broadly to the experience and that can be clearly defined, highlighted, and reinforced regularly.
- If your core values happen to provide you with the chance to create and use an acronym, awesome. If not, do not choose values based on the letters of the alphabet.
- Reevaluate your coaching philosophy consistently. Talk to other coaches, read books, and educate yourself on the most up-to-date best practices in coaching so that you can determine whether or not they fit you, your coaching style, and your philosophy. Be open to discussion and both internal and external dialogue that challenges your values and philosophy. The more you have tested it against different theories and scenarios, the more conviction you can build, the stronger your philosophy will be, and the more confidence you can find in yourself.
- Proudly share your philosophy with athletes' families and others invested in your program.
- Think bigger than you, the team, and maybe even the sport itself. Look to see where you can be making an impact on communities and the world of sports as a whole.

TIPS FOR SUPPORTING ATHLETES' SPIRITUAL WELLNESS

Athletes need and deserve to be able to look to their coach for consistency to help them find the calm amid the storm. You may or may not involve your athletes in the process of selecting the core values of the program, but they need your commitment to the structure and constant reinforcement of those values. The more devoted you are to your identity as a person and as a coach, the more they can trust you. To help support the spiritual wellness of athletes, consider the following:

- Express and demonstrate respect for all forms of spirituality. There are a multitude of places in which people find their meaning and passion in life, and athletes should know that their coaches support all viewpoints as valuable.

- Celebrate spirituality with your team in an inclusive manner. Help players to support one another and build everyone's understanding of others' traditions in a respectful, humble light. Show gratitude for athletes' willingness to share.
- Make T-shirts and signs, come up with an associated mantra, and repeat your values and beliefs often.
- While values should be demonstrated in all your behaviors, take the time to directly discuss moral decisions and appropriate actions, and help players to apply life lessons directly to sport. Sharing stories, discussing current events, and highlighting real life dilemmas faced by the team are some of the strategies to consider. If you want to help them develop character, you have to teach them explicitly—much like you would anything else in the game.
- Base your goals, team discussions, awards, and the like on core values. If you are going to tell athletes that these are the things that matter most, they should see that in your actions. For example, if attitude is a priority to you, discuss it every day, select a player of the week based on attitude *alone*, and help players to make the connection between performance and attitude.

A NOTE ON MOTIVATION

The best motivation always comes from within.

—*Michael Johnson*

As a coach, one of your primary roles will be to help athletes cultivate and manage motivation so that they can excel. When it comes to performance, motivation is essential for all athletes; however, the individual nature of motivation is important to keep in mind. The best coaches will adjust their coaching styles (not their identities or philosophies) to work most appropriately with each athlete. As they grow to know their players as people, coaches will grow increasingly effective in helping players to tap into their inspiration. Answers to the following questions may help coaches to create tailored motivational tactics for individual athletes: How motivated are they, and how do we know? Where do they get their motivation? Do they get their desire to play from outside influences (extrinsic factors) or does it come from within (intrinsic factors)?

There are benefits to extrinsic motivation, yet as the stage is set in athletics, the most impactful motivation is that which comes from within.[4] When it comes to athletes, the goal is to help them rely more on motivation from

APPLICATIONS IN COACH DEVELOPMENT:
IMPLEMENTING A COACHING PHILOSOPHY
AND ETHICAL DECISION-MAKING

All coaches benefit from an examination of their coaching philosophy, values, and motivation.[1] Regardless of their level of experience, it is essential that you discuss philosophy with coaches regularly. Help them build conviction in a working coaching philosophy that they can adapt as they progress. Your familiarity with their beliefs will guide the creation of a meaningful coach development plan. Ensuring that learning and growth aligns with and/or complements a coach's identity and values helps to maximize their commitment to *your* efforts. Who a coach is and what matters to them will be reflected in all of their coaching practices and therefore should be purposefully woven into coach development activities.[2]

There are many effective means for promoting integrity and ethics in coaching that may be employed by a coach developer. Exploring values and the influence of the specific sport context, along with connecting coach values to coaching behaviors, can help coaches to implement a values-based philosophy.[3] For example, if hard work is a core value, help coaches identify opportunities to challenge athletes' work ethic and demonstrate it as a priority. A well-built philosophy can help guide coaches through challenging dilemmas, yet explicitly practicing ethical decision-making is also a worthwhile endeavor. Thompson states that "case studies, role play, and perspective taking and reflection are some of the strategies suggested that could easily be implemented into the coach education curriculum."[4]

Notes

1. Melissa Thompson, "Ethical and Philosophical Grounding of Coaches," in *Coach Education Essentials: Your Guide to Developing Sport Coaches*, edited by Kristen Dieffenbach and Melissa Thompson (Champaign, IL: Human Kinetics, 2020), 17–34.

2. Cameron Kiosoglous, "Coach Education of Professional- and Olympic-Level Coaches," in *Coach Education Essentials: Your Guide to Developing Sport Coaches*, edited by Kristen Dieffenbach and Melissa Thompson (Champaign, IL: Human Kinetics, 2020), 155–70.

3. Thompson, "Ethical and Philosophical Grounding of Coaches."

4. Thompson, *Coach Education Essentials*, 25.

within and less on external factors or opinions. Your feedback is essential, especially in relation to skills and when the learning curve is steep. A coach's reinforcement and approval can be used to help athletes progress, but those actions are limited to short-term gains. The goal is to move that feedback from an external source to an empowered internal voice, so athletes are able to push *themselves* to do better.

STORIES OF *WINNING WELL* IN SPIRITUAL WELLNESS

Avery Longrie

Avery Longrie was a talented multisport athlete through his high school years. He developed a love for the game of rugby, went on to play for Grand Canyon University, and currently plays for a men's team. Playing sports helped him build confidence in his abilities, introduced him to one of his best friends, and led him to a relationship with God. Avery's story demonstrates how his coach helped him to form a connection to spiritual wellness, which propelled his success on the field.

> During my sophomore year of high school, my good friend Brendon moved to the area all the way from South Africa. He joined the football team and, to be honest, I wasn't a very big fan of him! I think it was because all the coaches were talking about how good of a football player he was, so I sorta saw him as competition. Brendon and his dad decided that it would be a good idea to put together a rugby team at the high school we were attending. I had never heard of rugby at that point, and it looked interesting, so I decided to join. That is where I met my coach, David, for the first time. As Brendon and I became good friends, I got to know David better too.
>
> David and Brendon's family was very religious, and since Brendon and I were good friends, they invited me to their youth group at Peoples' Church (which is still very dear to my heart). Not only did David's daughter run the youth group, David was one of the pastors at the church. I was not very religious prior to this. I had been to church a few times, but nothing serious. Over time, not only did my relationship with Brendon and David grow, my relationship with God grew as well. When they invited me to church camp, that is where my faith really started to take off.
>
> While building my faith, I was also learning lessons about commitment, hard work, and dedication in sports. Not everyone on our team was religious, but we all got into a circle and prayed before every game. David always emphasized

that no matter what happened on the field, our families would still love us and God would still love us. I personally believe that him putting that into our heads enabled us to play better as a team. We knew that no matter how bad of a game we played, no matter how many tackles we missed, everything would still be okay. The reassurance alone helped me to be able to leave it all on the field and not stress about what my coach was thinking or how I was playing. I was really able to focus on the task at hand and get the job done.

During my time playing for David, we won four or five state championships, half of our high school team made the all-star team, and our overall record was 90–2. To this day, I still carry that same mindset into everything that I do, helping to put 100 percent effort into each task. Not only did David help turn me into the best player I could be, he guided me through my religious journey, turning me into the best person I could be.

Asteria (Claure) Howard

Asteria (Claure) Howard earned numerous championships in track, running for both the Bolivian and Venezuelan national teams. Seeking opportunities to run throughout her life, she demonstrated incredible resilience driven by her motivation and faith. She has completed more than fifteen marathons and has established herself as a prominent master's-level competitor and coach. Guided by her spirituality, Asteria coaches athletes of all ages to maximize their wellness.

I grew up playing all the sports I could in my neighborhood. My favorite toy was a jump rope; jumping and playing was my world as a kid. My last year of high school we had a running coach visiting our school, trying to introduce us to track. He made us run in groups on the basketball court, and, sadly, I lost in my heat trying to pick up my shoes that had fallen off in the middle of the court. The consequence was that I didn't make the team and wasn't able to compete in a big race representing our school. It was a very sad moment for me to see the names of my schoolmates on the board with my name missing, even though I was considered the best athlete.

The day of the race came, and I went by myself to the stadium. It was my lucky day. It was my first time on a real track and there was one line empty just waiting for me! I started to yell at the coach, and the starting official heard my yelling. I jumped over the fence, put my regular shoes on the grass (because I didn't have running spikes) and there I was, barefoot, standing behind the line ready to run my first real 100-meter race. That was the start of my journey in running.

I became a part of the national team to represent my country, Bolivia, in the International (Bolivarian) Games. Our coach was not investing in me and I felt dismissed. I was disappointed and heartbroken. I just wanted to run, but I needed coaching. I decided to leave my country in search of better opportunities and different coaching. I arrived in Caracas, Venezuela, without any information—no friends, no relatives. I got to the track, started chatting a little bit with some runners, and thanks to God it worked. I started to compete almost every month in local, national, and international competitions.

Eventually, I was just running to keep in shape and in my mind I was telling myself that I was too old to compete anymore until I was introduced to the master's level. From that moment on, it felt like my life had been reborn in the master's.

In 1994, I had my first experience running the New York City Marathon. I hadn't done any long-distance training other than 5k runs on the track. I was praying and asking God to give me the opportunity to come back again to keep running the marathon for years to come. It was a big surprise to me to finish that first marathon. I even did it in 3:54 at thirty-four years old!

Returning to Venezuela from New York was hard. Things were totally different. We had Hugo Chaves as a president, and the economy of the country was declining each day. Because of the poor conditions, I decided to go back to Bolivia. I kept running and working as an elementary PE teacher. God had opened the door for me to make the Bolivian team to compete at the World Master's Championship in Buffalo, New York!

Initially, my visa was denied, but through a lot of effort, eventually I was able to get the visa and, thanks to God, my dream was becoming a reality. It took almost a week for me to make the trip, and during that time, my event had passed. The only way for me to be able to compete in Buffalo was to run the last event—the marathon. I barely had time to get to the village, leave my suitcase in the room, and go to the start of the marathon. I was doing this with no food, on terrible sleep, not speaking a word of English, just trying to make my dream a reality. The ultimate goal I had in mind was to finish the marathon representing my country, Bolivia.

When everything was over, I took a bus back to New York. I was by myself and was scared because I didn't know what, where, why, or how to do whatever I would do next. At the same time, I was open to new opportunities, so it was hard, but not hopeless. I stayed two days at the bus terminal, until God sent me one of his angels to help me find a room where I could stay.

My next step was to go to Central Park, looking for a group of Latin runners. God was with me all the time and he directed me to 90th and 5th Avenue. When I saw a group of runners, I went over and told them that I was also a runner. They helped me to register at New York Road Runners (NYRR) club for a race two days later and I won my age group. It would be the first of many trophies I have won from NYRR. After the race, I was introduced to the president of West Side Runners Club. I am now vice president and a coach, and our team has won twenty-six out of the last thirty-three Championships in Central Park. We're a team made up of all immigrants, different nationalities, different colors, all ages, speaking many languages. We run to represent our team with love and to be happy, healthy, and humble.

Through God's guidance, I have seen some amazing results in my coaching. I was able to work with Edison Peña, the survivor miner from Chile who came to run the NYC Marathon. Despite his doubts, he was able to finish. Marjorie Kagan, an eighty-two-year-old who wanted to run the NYC Marathon without any background in sports, spent five months training with me and was able to finish in 6:36:18. Isabel Trinidad, at eighty-two years-old, was in a wheelchair being moved by others like a baby. I helped her with stretches and exercises, and she's now able to walk and travel to visit her family.

When I look back on all my struggles, it is clear to me that with motivation, we can achieve our goals and dreams. My faith has contributed to my positive experiences as an athlete, and it serves as a guide for my current work as a coach. Remembering the times I had been let down by a coach or dismissed is one of the reasons I love to help anyone to reach their goals now. I thank God for the journey. It is a pleasure to do what I do and to be able to give to others what made such a difference for me.

6

Environmental Wellness

The more I have been involved in football, the more I realize that individual talent is minimized or maximized by the environment those blokes go into.

—Leigh Matthews

WHAT IS ENVIRONMENTAL WELLNESS IN THE CONTEXT OF SPORTS?

Humans do not operate in a vacuum. Our surroundings impact us in countless ways and can be so multilayered and complex that determining what is actually influencing us at any given time can be borderline impossible. Environmental wellness addresses the people and all of the characteristics within a space, be it a room, a building, a community, a region, the planet, or our universe. We each have an impact on the environment—at all of those levels.

In the world of sports, the environment encompasses the context in which you coach as well as the culture you create. In terms of the context, there are facilities and equipment, administrative supports or lack thereof, budgets and financial needs, and all the people within the system as a whole. It includes both the local community and the setting (school, club, organization, etc.) in which you coach, naturally bringing unique advantages and disadvantages. The support you receive will be greatly impacted by your context, as will the challenges you face.

In terms of the culture you create (or that is created on its own), characteristics of your program are constantly communicated to the people within the system as well as those outside of it. It is your identity, both that of your team and of *you* as a coach. As is the case for leaders in most sectors of society, coaches will be most personally pinned with the identity of the team. Environmental wellness in sports is defined by the wellness of the culture and what you do to maximize the positive aspects therein.

WHY DOES ENVIRONMENTAL WELLNESS MATTER IN THE WORLD OF ATHLETICS?

Coaches must manage a multitude of factors in the environment—some that can be controlled, others that can be influenced, and yet others that a coach couldn't impact if they spent all the effort in the world trying to do so. Regardless, your success, as well as that of the athletes and team, will be greatly impacted by the environment. It is essential that you learn as much as possible about the spaces and places in which you coach (and yes, the people are a part of all that).

When you are informed about the environment, you can make decisions about moving forward that make sense and maximize your progress and impact. In other words, having Olympic-level expectations for facilities in a low-budget community sports league may leave you feeling frustrated. If you are coaching athletes in a homogeneous, affluent, private club in the suburbs or in a rural community, much of your work on a daily basis may require a different approach than if you are coaching in an low-income, racially diverse, inner-city school. In general, to be effective, your coaching actions and decisions must be tailored to the environment and context in which you coach, or they have a decent chance of failure.[1] There will always be challenges, but if you approach those challenges with openness and honesty, you are much more likely to find a solution.

We all know stories about programs that have made a terrible or fantastic name for themselves based on their culture. By establishing an identity or program culture, you get to choose the legacy you leave behind in coaching. The first step is recognizing the impact of the environment, valuing its importance and influence, and then continuing to keep it in mind as you initiate change and development. You would never try to make your way through an obstacle course blindfolded if that wasn't specifically the challenge presented to you, so you should not try to coach within a vacuum when we all know things are just not that simple.

The environmental aspect of wellness tends to envelop all of the others. It includes connections and interactions between people, safety and vulnerability within the group, defining and staying true to your values, and positively and effectively responding to successes and failures. Environmental wellness provides the energy within the physical space. It is dictated by the culture, and people can feel it when they enter the room. Practices in a positive environment are vibrant. They are high energy and focused. Communication from the coach is purposeful and uplifting. The space itself has been loved and cared for. Players are able to give 100 percent effort because they know they are respected as unique individuals. There is a shared language that may not mean much to an outsider but is used consistently by the group. There are expectations of greatness that permeate each activity and that push all players appropriately. One would be hard-pressed to find a winning program that lacks a thoughtfully constructed environment. If we want to win games, meets, or matches, building a winning culture is essential.

PROBLEM: WE ARE TRYING TO COACH WITH BLINDERS ON!

When it comes to environmental wellness, sports programs run the gamut from optimal to abysmal. There are coaches who have taken great care in considering all the different factors within their environments. They make the most of their logistical constraints, including finances, facilities, equipment, access to pool or ice time, ability to build a coaching staff, community demographics, athlete priorities, parent engagement, and the list goes on. Those coaches establish a winning culture driven by the pride of the individuals within the program—pride in their true identity, inclusive of everything that identity entails. The coaches who embrace their environment, take care of what they have, and guide athletes specifically based on who they are and where they come from have the best chances of success.[2]

On the flip side, unfortunately, some coaches almost literally beat their heads into a wall trying to impart a system they want to see come to fruition in a setting where it is not supported. Having goals and ideals in mind is fantastic, but so is being realistic. In the world of education, we talk about meeting students where they are to be most successful,[3] and overall, that is also what we hope to see in relation to environmental wellness in coaching.

In programs that struggle with environmental wellness, the establishment of culture is often left to chance or carelessly built. For example, it may not be athlete centered, inclusive, safe, and/or uplifting. The variety of struggles faced by such programs is limitless, yet such problems are avoidable when environmental wellness is made a priority.

A NOTE ON FEASIBILITY AS IT RELATES TO ENVIRONMENTAL WELLNESS
In relation to maximizing environmental wellness, a few barriers that you may encounter include, but are not limited to, the following:

- Known factors in an environment such as poverty, violence, and injustice may hinder the wellness of specific individuals and groups.[4]
- Different spaces are welcoming or unsafe for people based on their intersectional identities—this could be within your team, between teams, on the road, at restaurants, and so on.
- The symbols, signs, and messages that are conveyed in spaces may impact athletes in very different ways.
- Language barriers may surface in any setting for athletes and/or families.

While this list is not exhaustive, taking the time to acknowledge potential barriers to wellness is imperative.

Environmental wellness in sports builds a consistently pleasant, supportive environment that promotes holistic well-being, engaging with the community, and embracing diversity.

WHERE ARE YOU NOW?
1. How do you feel about your current environmental wellness?
2. How do you feel about the environmental wellness of the athletes you coach?
3. How much of a priority is it for you to support your athletes' environmental wellness?

4. How well-informed and prepared do you feel to help maximize environmental wellness in the athletes you coach?

5. How do your personal and coaching practices support or detract from your athletes' environmental wellness?

TIPS FOR SUPPORTING YOUR OWN ENVIRONMENTAL WELLNESS

To ensure you are at your best, bringing your best energy into a space, acting with integrity, and helping to build a strong culture, you must account for all aspects of your own wellness. Universal considerations for enhancing personal environmental wellness include the following:

- Take the time each season to relearn as much as you can about the environment. Even if this is your thirty-eighth year in this position, whether you like it or not, things change. You may have lost or gained something in relation to facilities, equipment, support staff, and/or athletes. All of the people involved will continue to develop and change over time, so even if everything appears to be the same, undoubtedly it is not.

- Pay attention to how different environments affect wellness, for better or worse. Gaining awareness of the impact on yourself and others is a crucial step in mitigating any negative impact. Take it all in and focus on the things you can influence.

- Manage your stress so that you are not bringing unnecessary negative or overbearing energy into team meetings, practices, or competitions. Energy is contagious—in both productive and harmful ways.

- Take care of the environments you inhabit. Keep things clean, organized, and functional. You don't need to obsessively try to control everything in your spaces, but do your part to maintain healthy and effective environments for yourself. Demonstrate professionalism to others through your environments and the manner in which you present yourself.

- Promote environmental wellness through communication with officials, opponents, coaching staff, team members, parents, fans, and media. When you have built a culture of which you feel proud, you will feel it every time you step onto the field. While demonstrating this level of consistency may be challenging, embrace those challenges, and through your efforts, you can truly promote your program as a whole.

- Ask for feedback from trusted individuals about the culture and identity of your program. It can be difficult to hear sometimes, but take advantage of diversity in opinions. Knowing what you and your program are communicating to others can assist you in building the culture you desire. It can also help to highlight both strengths and weaknesses.
- Outside of coaching activities and your sport environments, to the public, you are still Coach So-and-So. If your public messages or behaviors are not representative of the program you hope to build, it can be detrimental to your reputation as a coach and your ability to establish a respectful culture within your program.
- In your environment, emphasize your passion while fostering the joy that your sport provides.

TIPS FOR SUPPORTING ATHLETES' ENVIRONMENTAL WELLNESS

Environmental wellness is so comprehensive that anything you do to support wellness in athletes will have a positive impact on the environment. The following are a few other ideas to consider that haven't been addressed just yet:

- Use purposeful planning and thoughtful behaviors and messaging to create and/or support the culture that you want to see in your program. Culture will develop in a group whether we take the reins or not, and when we just let things happen, there's no telling what we will get.[5] If you want players to exhibit what matters most to the program, they must not have any questions about the expectations and characteristics that should be displayed by everyone. Your messaging needs to be abundantly clear.
- Consider the routines you employ as central to supporting your culture— they will either reinforce or detract from your core values. Establishing routines may take more of an investment in time initially, but it is worth it in the end. Routines let players know what to expect, promote comfort and confidence, and help to form the picture of who you are as a group (for example, practice plans that consistently begin with opportunities for team building).
- Provide players with positively stated, clear, concise, specific feedback about exactly what they did well or what they should do differently. Employing productive feedback is a critical coaching skill that enhances performance, influences the environment, and impacts individuals' wellness. Saying

"good job" is nice, but it doesn't tell athletes anything they need to know about what you hope to see replicated. In a similar vein, telling players *not* to do something can create confusion and ambiguity while typically leading them straight to those actions you are hoping they will avoid.[6] It may take practice to maximize the positive impact of your feedback for athletes, and there are a variety of methods worth exploring.

- Within all the spaces that you and the athletes occupy, guide players to be organized, take care of equipment, and keep things clean. Whether you have all the best equipment and facilities in the world or you have very little to work with, it is important to teach players not to take anything for granted and to communicate your expectations around such behaviors. This is about building pride in the program and in personal actions. You can show and feel a lot of pride in something when you collectively take care of it. In all of your team spaces, on the road, traveling, at restaurants, out in the community, and the like, teach your athletes to leave a place better than they found it.

- Promote all athletes' contributions to inclusive, supportive energy in the environment.

- Ensure that athletes know they are loved and appreciated as people, not just competitors. When players feel safe in an environment, they can be vulnerable and authentic, which is essential to help them to reach their potential. Knowing that mistakes are expected and that support will be provided is vital for athletes' learning and development.[7]

- Seek out opportunities to contribute to the community. On your own or with your athletes, when you are making a positive impact on the community at any level, athletes respect that engagement and recognize that you are not just feigning interest. Not only does service help to teach numerous life lessons, it is a fantastic team-building activity and can greatly contribute to rallying support in all forms for your program.[8] Additionally, engaging in the local community, school, or organization in which you coach gives you an opportunity to get to know more about where you coach and the people around you.

- Be a steward of your sport. Help to promote the game itself by demonstrating respect for everyone involved, including opponents, officials, and fans. Discuss current issues and stories related to your sport with athletes, and venture into other sports as well. If possible, take the time to go to or watch a game or competition together. It can be at any level of the sport—higher, lower, or similar to the level you coach. Showing appreciation for the game is contagious and helps to foster respect for others and a love of the game.

- Finally, help guide parents in contributing to your program identity in a constructive way. When you meet with them to start the season, discuss your expectations for the crowd at your games and let them know how they can positively contribute. Get them involved in promoting your culture. Much like with your players, messages to parents about your priorities and the program identity should be repetitive, clear, and easy to grasp.

APPLICATIONS IN COACH DEVELOPMENT: ESTABLISHING A LEARNER-CENTERED ENVIRONMENT AND PROVIDING EFFECTIVE FEEDBACK

Setting the stage for coaches to learn requires purposeful application of theories of andragogy.[1] Starting with a strong relational foundation between the coach and coach developer, create an organized, motivating, and welcoming physical space. Such an environment is conducive to active learning and authentic coach engagement. Because adults desire involvement in the planning and implementation of their own learning, are guided by past experiences, and are motivated to solve problems, the goal is to create a space that feels empowering to coaches. For example, arranging seating to promote conversation and using clean whiteboards and large Post-It notes on the walls support hands-on learning and a motivating, learner-centered environment.[2]

Environments are substantially impacted by the quality of the leader's communication. In the teaching and coaching world, much of that communication comes in the form of feedback. Build your skills in providing multiple forms of feedback so that you can maintain a learner-centered environment for all coaches and maximize the effectiveness of your teaching. Not only will your delivery of feedback to coaches impact their development, it will serve as a model for effective coaching strategies.

It is essential to also explicitly guide coaches in providing meaningful feedback to athletes so they can establish a strong learning environment as well.[3]

Providing quality, productive feedback takes concerted effort, skill, and practice. A variety of approaches are supported in the literature; however, feedback should always be intentional and purposefully matched to the type and complexity of the skill being taught as well as the skill level of the learner. Examining various feedback methods and their applications may serve as an integral learning experience for coaches. As Matthew A. Grant explains, "Understanding the multiple types of feedback and how they can be used in practice enhances knowledge, learning, and performance by an athlete. In short, the importance of feedback cannot be overstated. . . . Coach developers should help coaches differentiate what these types of feedback look like in practice."[4] For example, guiding coaches to ask questions and pull insight and perspective from athletes as opposed to pushing information is one method to consider. It can be employed with athletes who exhibit varying levels of competence and its purpose is multilayered. Questioning helps athletes to internalize learning and the physical execution of a skill, while enhancing intrinsic motivation.[5]

Notes

1. International Council for Coaching Excellence, "Facilitation Handbook: Introduction to Facilitation Skills," presented at the 2018 ICCE/USCCE Coach Developer Academy, Orlando, FL, 2018; Malcolm S. Knowles and Associates. *Andragogy in Action: Applying Modern Principles of Adult Learning* (San Francisco: Jossey-Bass, 1984).

2. International Council for Coaching Excellence, "Facilitation Handbook: Introduction to Facilitation Skills."

3. Matthew A. Grant, "Coach Instruction for Effective Athlete Instruction," in *Coach Education Essentials: Your Guide to Developing Sport Coaches*, edited by Kristen Dieffenbach and Melissa Thompson (Champaign, IL: Human Kinetics, 2020), 67–89.

4. Grant, *Coach Education Essentials*, 76.

5. University of Washington, Center for Leadership in Athletics, Center for Leadership in Athletics, University of Washington: Where Education, Sport, & Research Converge (2018), http://uwcla.uw.edu/; International Council for Coaching Excellence, "Facilitation Handbook: Introduction to Facilitation Skills."

STORIES OF *WINNING WELL* IN ENVIRONMENTAL WELLNESS

Camille Adana

Growing up in a tumultuous environment, Camille Adana found solace in sports. She was able to cope with the realities of poverty and drug abuse through the strength of the village that surrounded her. The environment created for her by her coaches and mentors greatly impacted Camille's overall wellness and served as an inspiration. As a result, creating a safe place for athletes to hold themselves accountable is truly her passion in coaching.

I am the kid that needed structure and sports to help me overcome adversity. I believe all people go through hardships in their lifetimes, and learning how to cope with stress should be structured into the regimen of our lives starting at a very young age. My family was consistently being uprooted due to alcoholism, drug abuse, physical abuse, and poverty. I went to six grade schools and didn't really know much about anything other than survival. My mom randomly found a duplex across the street from Brooklyn Park. I remember the day we moved in, I sprinted over to the park and stumbled upon a game called tetherball. I literally fell into play. I had such a blast pounding that ball against other kids. It was the first time I felt a competitive spirit. Who would have thought that tetherball in a public park would introduce me to the world of athletics?

I was drawn to everything that happened in the park. An equipment shack opened up, free lunches were given out, and random kids from the neighborhood played all kinds of sports. At the time, I wasn't yet aware of anything regarding organized sport, yet because I could check out a basketball, it became one of my go-to games. The park had a regimented program when it came to both equipment and scheduling times for play. There were basketball, tennis, golf, ping-pong, mush ball, and wiffle ball tournaments and competitions. Within the structure, there were rules, etiquette, and boundaries around sportsmanship. All of these rules were respected because of the efforts of the park director—Craig—the adult in charge.

Craig was matter-of-fact and created a sense of structure at the park. I remember thinking to myself, "I cannot disrespect this guy." From the day I met him and learned about everything the park had to offer, I leaned into every physical activity known to man. The park was the most magical place. I felt free, authentic, and in my own skin when I was there. One day, I was so authentic that I said the f-word while playing ping-pong. All of a sudden, here comes the park director, and it was consequence time. My game was an automatic forfeit.

I had to sit behind the shack at a picnic table and rewrite the same sentence, repeatedly apologizing for my mistake.

This is how the story changes when it comes to respect, expectations, and structure in an environment outside of my home. I didn't know that these types of expectations could happen at a park, but they did. Even though my family had its dysfunction, my parents expected respect toward adult figures or there would be a consequence. Because of this, when Craig held me accountable, I embraced the expectation. I was disappointed in myself because I disappointed him with my words. I was blessed to have had parents, along with a park director, that expected respect. If I didn't have the supportive environment, plus sports, in my life, I wouldn't be here today. While growing up and playing at the park every summer, I became a role model (and consequently, watched my profanity). I didn't want to get into trouble. While I was being active and learning that I was a good athlete, I was also checking my behavior because of the expectations Craig had in the park.

Craig observed my natural talent when I played and decided to take on a supportive role financially: He paid all my participation fees. The opportunity he helped me to realize allowed me to learn more about environments and expectations through organized sports.

In retrospect, my commitment in the beginning was very nonchalant; I didn't realize what I was getting into. I was having fun and being somewhat competitive, with coaches infusing their expectations onto me. I guess they saw my raw talent and wanted to invest in coaching me with high expectations. I felt like I was bouncing around from environment to environment with all these adults telling me what to do, expecting me to be respectful, responsible, and represent the community. It was crazy how, in time, my life became a huge commitment to sports.

It got to the point that random parents in the sport seasons took a mentorship role in my life as well. They would pick me up for practices and games and hold me to their expectations. I would be ready, they would drive up, and I would go. I don't know how much my parents knew or how any of this went down because they were very busy trying to pay the bills and put food on the table. I was blessed because even though they couldn't watch me play or support me financially, they allowed other adults to hold me accountable. They allowed me to participate on every team and to play at Brooklyn Park around the clock. Even though I come from a tumultuous background, they did the right thing trusting the village to play a role in raising me as a young girl.

Brooklyn Park opened up every summer, and I could not wait for my time there. I loved school, but Brooklyn Park embodied freedom to me—freedom to run, play, get better, compete, and to do so with the utmost respect to everyone there. I remember a time when my parents were struggling to pay rent because the rent kept increasing over the years. I begged my mom to stay. I cried at the thought of leaving our neighborhood. I babysat just to help my mom with bills. I never wanted to leave my safe haven, the place I called home. This place was a treasure. It was a part of my heart and taught me the meaning of being an athlete for life. Where would I be today if my mom didn't choose the duplex across the street from Brooklyn Park? I don't think sport would have been introduced to me. Behold the power of an environment set up for kids with a mentor as a park director that cared about the bigger picture in life. Such a miracle.

The next thing you know, I am starting high school, and shit got real, real quick. The expectations, grade checks, school attendance, 24/7 commitment, and the breakdown of seasons—WTF? I felt like I constantly had coaches coming at me about the importance of academics, commitment, and staying above the influence while kicking my ass physically. My high school coaches created a consistent environment—an environment of role-modeling and high expectations for all athletes. There were no "ifs," "ands," or "buts." I knew what to expect in the fall, winter, spring, and summer, and I craved that structure. Being an athlete was my story, and I was literally committed to two sports a season from the ninth grade until college. I was on the go, committed, and supported throughout high school because of Craig and my coaches. I had intrinsic motivation to play in college and be the first person to graduate from high school in my immediate family, and I can analyze the impact now, but at the time, I was just doing what I was told to do.

All of the environments in my life helped contribute to my success. My home was tough, but I was loved immensely. I have so much respect for all the adults that somehow lined up perfectly for me from sixth grade through my college playing days. My mother, father, park director, and coaches all carried the same expectations and love for me.

In my adult life, I have coached and implemented the same consistent, safe environments for my students and athletes. All are aware of the connectedness you can feel when an environment is structured, secure, and full of accountability. When this is known, the safety of opening up and showing your real emotional self happens naturally because of the overall safety you feel in the environment with a caring adult.

It is critical for adult figures to realize the impact they can make on young adults. Every athlete is on a personal journey. They are just looking for structure, consistency, and positive reinforcement. Motivation is different in every athlete, but when a coaching staff sees their athletes as people and wants to guide and give structure as well as provide positive, specific feedback, you will see motivation shoot through the roof. It is powerful. There is love in an environment like this.

I am so thankful for my parents for having high expectations around respect. I feel blessed to have randomly met Craig, whom I adore to this day. I am honored that I was set up to be able to accept my high school coaches and their expectations. I feel well today because I know how to set up an environment for myself and others that is full of respect. I truly believe in the village that raised me, the consistent expectations they maintained in the environment, and how they prepared me for life and living well.

JOSH CARLSON

When Josh Carlson first stepped into coaching Special Olympics basketball, he had no idea what to expect beyond an opportunity to give to the game. He quickly and unexpectedly found himself in a sports environment like none he had ever encountered before (and not just because of the team's undefeated record). The athletes' effort and dedication have changed his view not only of sports, but of the world. Maintaining the unique and supportive nature of the environment to uphold all athletes' wellness is Josh's top priority.

Being involved with Special Olympics has been one of the best experiences of my life. I love basketball . . . and so do these athletes! One of our biggest goals is to create an environment where people with disabilities of all ages can feel welcomed with respect and love. I would have never imagined how much I would gain from my involvement with Special Olympics. It's easy to get caught up in the whirlwind of everything going on in the world, but for a few hours every Saturday, I put aside everything else for hoops and high-fives.

Coaching should be about mentorship and caring, and we work to ensure that everyone feels that at all times in the gym. We work hard and we play to win, but it is never at the sacrifice of inclusion and good sportsmanship. I am inspired by the athletes' effort along with their love for the game and one another. I have never seen anything like this in sports. The athletes have certainly taught me more than I could ever teach them.

Efforts to create an inclusive environment are supported and even at times guided by our athletes. These athletes understand deep down that the individual is not the most important part of the equation. They know how to authentically empathize with one another—with their teammates and even their opponents. I've learned that all of these athletes are simply seeking recreational peace. They just want to come here and compete and not be looked at weird or judged. They want to play and feel okay while doing it. In this environment, they can play without judgment from others. Their disabilities aren't looked at as a hindrance or a difference, and there's really a lot of community in that. It's different from what I have always seen in sports, and it's honestly been life-changing for me.

What's cool about basketball, in particular, is that it's accessible to everyone. They love it when you learn their skill sets because you can truly help them as individuals. They know that they matter to you. There's something they can all do to engage in the sport at their own level, even if that means just holding the ball in a specific way. What really motivates them is that because it's a team sport, we can all, in theory, do it together. That possibility is what gets people to come back every week. A catch made, a dribble produced, and a shot put up is really a massive task, and when they achieve it, it's something spectacular that we all celebrate. We're constantly looking forward to the next week because we know we've left something on the table to improve or try again.

One of the craziest parts of this is that we only practice once a week and compete one time a year. These athletes are just as passionate about the game as any of us and probably more so. Imagine only being able to play one day a week when you have so much passion for the game! Being together in the gym is literally what the athletes live for, and although they're adults, they have to wait for someone to give them a ride to practice. For a squad that doesn't get to compete other than once a year, I get a level of commitment out of them that you can't believe.

I've come to realize that out of every athlete in every sport at every level, Special Olympics athletes bring an energy that all coaches dream of having in their athletes. They get to compete just one time each year, and how they manage that blows my mind. To not have a sourness about you on game day if you didn't win or it just wasn't your day when you've worked so hard all year?! They aren't worried about what they look like; they're worried about having a great day, and they want that for everyone else, too. They go out of their way to pick their teammates up and to make the most of the game—every time. Their attitudes are inspiring, and the way they're supported by the environment is something we can all learn from in sports.

I feel so lucky to be able to coach Special Olympics athletes. I learn something every week from the athletes that literally changes my life. I imagine that would be hard to find in any other environment. It's given me a whole new idea about how to approach athleticism, competition, empathy, and love. They always impress me because even though we're still in the sports scene, and they will give everything they can to win, there is zero ego. They've faced more adversity than most people can imagine in life. They go through their days seeing the world the same way as we do, but they do it while being constantly belittled and struggling to do things that we take for granted. So when we get here in this community, in this environment, everything the athletes do feels like the greatest thing in the world. Within five seconds you're high-fiving everyone because what is happening at any moment is the best. It's truly about a pure love of the game. I love to do this more than anything. I feel very fortunate to coach in this environment. It has absolutely, 100 percent, changed my life for the better.

7

Inclusion and Wellness

Although it does not stand alone as a dimension of wellness, embracing holistic wellness requires a conscious, purposeful focus on inclusion.[1] From individual to systemic levels, supporting participants of all identities demands intentional inclusive actions, particularly on the part of leaders. As a result, coaches and others are consistently encouraged to create inclusive environments, yet there is limited discussion regarding the logistics of enacting such efforts. While not exhaustive, some of the practices that help form the foundation for inclusive sports programs are presented in this chapter.

It's undeniable that we live in a society plagued by a variety of inequities, and sports are no exception. In fact, we can often look to athletics as a prime example to demonstrate our culture's biggest issues and most oppressive systems at work.[2] This section will address just two primary areas of focus which pertain to all coaching roles—race, ethnicity, or color and gender or LGBTQ2+ identity. Regardless of the context and diversity on any team, coaches are positioned to minimize oppression and simultaneously improve wellness for all. Due to the nature of intersectionality, we must acknowledge the role that *all* aspects of identity play in the sports scene, and the discussion here simply provides a starting point. An authentic investment in wellness requires building athletic environments on a foundation of inclusion and literally leveling the playing field.

BIPOC (BLACK, INDIGENOUS, AND PEOPLE OF COLOR)

I'm not concerned with your liking or disliking me . . . all I ask is that you respect me as a human being.

—*Jackie Robinson*

Sports are complex and powerful, a multidimensional component of our culture. They provide us ample opportunities to connect with one another, to celebrate both our differences and our similarities. They allows us a physical outlet and countless chances to grow together in relation to all dimensions of wellness. Sports themselves promote inclusion, diversity, and unity naturally, but the systems we have created to allow for participation in athletics certainly do not support those causes. The opportunities that *should* be available in athletics to all are not.[3] As is the case with much of our society, BIPOC (Black, Indigenous, and people of color) communities are disproportionately impacted by the harmful system that has been built in sports, limiting their wellness potential.

With debates around paying college athletes, efforts to expand access in sports leagues and clubs, and conversations around the use of sports as a platform for social justice, it is clear that athletics have by no means escaped the impacts of systemic racism in American culture. Many athletes are treated as objects ("dumb jocks") used for monetary advancement or the success of an organization while their holistic identity as individuals is devalued. This rings particularly true for athletes of color.[4] Athletes, coaches, administrators, officials, and fans all have different experiences in the sports world based on the color of their skin. While there are efforts to improve the system, the decision makers in athletics are still almost all white, and opportunities are far from equitable.

Although the sports system is corrupt, it is not beyond repair. There are many different clubs, organizations, and individuals committed to maximizing opportunities and improving the experience for BIPOC communities. It may take some creativity and nontraditional thinking, but it is absolutely worth every effort made. When we aren't afraid to truly embrace inclusion and examine all of our actions through an equity lens, systemic change is possible. To prioritize wellness, there must be a shift that permeates the entire world of sports—one that values all participants, at all levels, as essential to our creation of the best version of the system that we have yet to see. While addressing the struggles created for marginalized populations, we must also celebrate their contributions. This work will be ongoing and continuous as we strive to dismantle racism and prejudices within society, and wellness-enhancing sports environments are a great place to proceed with the movement.

Racial discrimination directly impacts the wellness of everyone involved in sports, including those in leadership roles. On individual, organizational, and community levels, there is much to be done to encourage and support Black coaches and administrators in addition to athletes.[5]

BIPOC PERSPECTIVE ON *WINNING WELL*

Coach Blue

Coach Blue played basketball at a small college and after graduating started a career in social services. He has spent the past twenty years promoting diversity, equity, and inclusion through his work. Coach Blue shares his experiences as a Black coach of primarily Black athletes and advice for enhancing wellness through an inclusive environment.

> I have coached for a long time in different environments. I will speak to being a Black head coach in a state where I am one of only a handful of Black head coaches, period. When I took the job, I told the school I was going to need administrative support. I told them they would need to support me as a Black coach and that I would be there for the Black and brown students as well as the white students. I said, "Look around—there is no one that looks like me, and you are going to have to have my back." My coaching staff is all African American as well and our team has grown increasingly diverse. I am proud of the inclusive culture we have established.
>
> I definitely see and feel bias and racism as a coach in many different environments. Our staff is oftentimes judged differently than our peers. At times I feel like we have to work twice as hard to get respect from others. Our team looks different than most opposing teams. We take pride in having a top program, but when coaches in the league vote for annual awards, we are often left questioning if implicit and/or explicit bias plays a significant role in those selections. We want our kids to feel respected. There is a model of accountability and respect that should be employed for everyone, but that is definitely not what we experience.

Here are just a few examples of the inequities I have seen in the sports arena. . . . It is common for refs to treat my players differently than white athletes. I had an official tell me, "Your players are intimidating, and your guys present themselves as rude and disrespectful." It feels very similar to the way discipline is disproportionately handled with our Black students throughout the United States. The discrimination can be glaringly obvious. Our 6-foot-8, 240-pound Black player is treated differently than similarly sized white opponents because of his physical appearance. As for my interactions, often there will be an opposing coach who will run out onto the floor towards a referee and nothing happens, but I ask for an explanation during a timeout, and am completely dismissed. The discrepancies are even noticeable in the stands. Officials and athletic directors interpret the crowd differently with Black parents and fans. They will say they are just trying to get the crowd under control, but there is a biased reaction based on the race of the fans. Even administrators need to be educated. I have to tell them the Black people are just cheering, not being rude. There is a tendency to stereotype Black women in particular as loud, scary, and intimidating, but they are actually just passionate. If people knew those fans, they would know it isn't anger or disrespect. Those are some of the inequities and biases involved for players, coaches, and families.

From the top down, bias and racism play a substantial role in coaching and the sports environment. My team has experienced a ton of racism in our league because of our demographics. The instilled, taught racism and language used by other programs is a culture that is set. The problems we have faced have been immense and will not change if education doesn't happen in all communities. Inclusion as a base must be built into the culture.

I know you have heard this before: "I am not racist; I don't see color." Well, then, you don't see me. You don't see that I am different. I want you to see my color. I want you to see all of your players' color, recognize their lived experiences, and love them for who they are. Most of the time this doesn't happen because of the lack of education and misunderstanding of systemic racism and equity. Systems are in place that impact athletes long before they get to me. Race has played such a significant role in this, and that is why it is important that the person in front of the kid reflects who they are serving. I think a white coach could still support Black athletes, but they have to see where the race and equity paths cross. I think coaches need to have a deep understanding of the trauma our young Black and brown students are going through and what they are up against.

How does a coach walk with their athletes compassionately, support them, and love them authentically? I think this is such an important consideration as a coach, especially a white coach working with Black athletes. You cannot coach an athlete fully unless you know who they are, the environment they come from, and what their experiences have been. Aspiring to have a diverse staff helps coaches work together to connect with the athletes and to show support for all the athletes in the program. It is about loving one another, and it is demonstrated in the way we structure our programs.

Inclusion is the foundation of everything I do. In our program, we try to implement educational experiences to spark conversations regularly. A couple years ago, we had a talk about kneeling during the national anthem. Some of our athletes chose to participate and others did not. It was an opportunity for discussion and to empower youth to use their voice and to build confidence. This is our job as coaches and educators—to inspire empathy and help athletes build their capacity to lead. My vision is to teach my players the difference between success and significance. Success is an individually focused endeavor, and significance is what you do to impact your team, school, and community. It is important to foster that growth, not just the skill of putting the ball in the basket. These are the aspects of the culture that promote a healthy environment.

When it comes to inclusion, there has to be major training. We need to educate our teachers, coaches, administrators, athletic directors, and the others involved in sports to promote empathy because there is a total disconnect. People really need to look at the structures in the environment when they say they want diversity. They need to consider what the investment in diversity involves. It's not just money, but time, talent, and authentic commitment that should be dedicated to supporting everyone's wellness. You have to recondition yourself entirely to support a community that is inclusive and diverse.

GENDER AND LGBTQ2+ (LESBIAN, GAY, BISEXUAL, TRANSGENDER, QUEER/QUESTIONING, TWO-SPIRIT, AND OTHER SEXUAL ORIENTATIONS AND GENDER IDENTITIES)

We currently do not have a sports system built for girls. If we did, it would look very different—and it would benefit everyone.

—Lauren Fleshman

An important distinction to make is that "female" is a term often used to refer to the primary and secondary sex characteristics of a human body (i.e., biological sex), while the terms "girl" and "woman" address the social construct of gender. Sports have traditionally been divided and continue to be divided on the men's sports/women's sports binary, which causes issues. It seems the intention was to create a biological divide, but our culture and the broad application of gender and gender norms have muddied the waters significantly. Debates around gender and biological sex continue today, and it is clear we have a long way to go in clarifying what this all means in a sports environment. Significant efforts have been made by advocates that continue in this aspect of sports culture. Hopefully we will get to the point where all genders are welcome in all sports, sooner rather than later.

This section is intended to be inclusive of all genders. In that quest, it is essential to acknowledge some of the stereotypes that relate to gender socialization and cultural expectations. It is of utmost importance that we make the social construction of gender clear and bring to light the fact that we are isolating gender outside of numerous very important factors including race, religion, socioeconomic status, sexual orientation, and so on.

One of the most influential aspects of the environment will always be the people along with the societal expectations imposed on those people. This topic should be managed very carefully because it can be easy to succumb to the gender stereotypes upon which we were raised. As athletes and coaches, it is imperative that we do our part to help support the girls, women, and gender-diverse athletes who are maneuvering their way through the world of sports.

Much of this section will be devoted to girls and women because of the archaic practices that prevent gender equity in athletics and hinder the potential for holistic wellness. This is not to downplay the oppressed experience of gender-diverse and trans athletes, a population that is seeking a place in sports in general. Because our promotion of anything beyond the standard binary is so young, this section will primarily focus on issues with the binary itself. Coaches play an influential role in being able to stand up for all genders and supporting wellness for all as the world of sports negotiates related issues.

Girls and women athletes are regularly dismissed as lesser and encounter numerous microaggressions that indicate the inferiority of their experience. Such behaviors can be extremely hurtful and damaging to overall wellness. If we trace the history of sports back to their roots, we find no place for girls or women. This discrimination continues to rear its ugly head in many ways.

Over time, we have seen a gradual increase in opportunities for girls and women. Due to biological factors, along with societal and cultural influences, since the beginning of sport, we have separated the genders on a binary basis. For this reason, coaches who employ a gender-inclusive lens—which values the experiences of cisgender, transgender, and nonbinary people—show us the importance of approaching this subject with compassion and an open mind.

To the detriment of individuals and society, most people have been socialized by gender expectations (that depth always varying from one person and/ or culture to the next). For many individuals, socialization into gender roles begins before they are even born. Typically, there is an expectation in society that men and boys will be physical and unemotional, and that they will value competition above collaboration, to name a few sports-related stereotypes. On the flip side, women and girls are expected to be cooperative, highly emotional, and standoffish or unaggressive. How much this has been socialized into each individual varies. One thing is certain: there is more difference within any individual gender than we tend to find between genders, and that factor alone makes this topic incredibly complex.[6]

Whether we like it or not, there are some deeply ingrained behaviors and beliefs that we may need to overcome as coaches and that we have the opportunity to help others see through as well. Building a more inclusive environment starts with a critical and deep assessment of your own identity and beliefs, along with an examination of their origins. The more you strive to understand yourself and athletes of all genders, the more you can promote holistic wellness. When given the opportunity to support, for example, emotional expression from boys and men or commitment to competition with girls and women, take full advantage. In those moments, you are seeing the human and authentic side of that person and can contribute to minimizing some of the gender role socialization that has built such inhibiting inequities in sports.

Dependent upon the competitive level at which you coach, the amount of difference you may find between boys/men and girls/women will vary. How you recognize and communicate successes and failures may need to be adjusted. For example, it may not be in your best interest to call out a boy or man for his excellent cooperation, although that cooperation greatly contributes to team success. For some boys or men, doing so would be fantastic; for others it could be humiliating. Typically, that type of recognition for girls or women is welcomed, but dependent upon the person, may not be the case.[7] Being cognizant of the socialization that has potentially occurred for each athlete, you will be most effective if you know them all as individuals and use that understanding to ensure an inclusive environment.

With girls, women, and gender-diverse athletes, keep in mind that their participation in sports alone may be frowned upon. Their access to opportunities is typically limited and the importance and value of their experience downplayed. Even today, girls and women are still affected by gender roles that keep them on the sidelines when they would love nothing more than to be participating. Athletes who identify with genders outside of the binary are just now starting to find their place and will certainly need our help in promoting their opportunities. Again, the experience will vary from one athlete to the next, but acknowledging the strength it may take for any one athlete to even step on the field of play is important. Not all athletes have been given equitable opportunities, and the impacts on wellness are understandably far-reaching and vary greatly from one individual to the next. The lack of support and discouraging messages repeated by society, based on gender, are disheartening.

Regardless of the gender of the athletes you coach, you are responsible for changing that messaging and creating a more inclusive environment. It is especially important to consider the explicit and implicit messages that coaches are conveying to athletes in boys' and men's sports about the participation of girls and women in athletics. Only when participants in boys' and men's sports start talking about girls' and women's sports as equally important and valuable to their own can we start to break down the barriers that have permeated sports culture, for example, asking boys and men to name their favorite professional female soccer player. Your actions, words, and attitudes will either perpetuate stereotypes and exclusionary systems or help to slowly break them down.

Finally, it is pertinent to acknowledge the presence of women in the world of coaching and athletic leadership. As is the case with almost all aspects of society, we see a disproportionate number of women in leadership roles along with insufficient support and inequities in pay, opportunities, and treatment. The impact on sports is compounded by the fact that athletics are and have historically been a masculine domain of society. The US Women's Soccer team has done a fantastic job of bringing some of these inequities into main-stream media. There are initiatives within many organizations to promote women and their experience in coaching (for example, WeCOACH);[8] how-ever, whether blatant or subtle, explicit or implicit, the world of sports is laced with all sorts of discriminating messages, practices, and barriers for women.

Some of the struggles we face in the world of athletics are perpetuated by the discrepancy in the number of women as opposed to men who hold leader-ship roles. For example, within the context of a culture that doesn't typically support emotional expression in men, how can we teach athletes to express themselves if most coaches are men? Obviously, there are exceptions, and we should all be grateful for the boys and men who have the courage to express emotion. Expanding the coaching profession to include more women may help in this respect as well as many others—diversity builds strength. When we look at women of color, in particular, the numbers quickly become abys-mal. As of 2019, only 42.1 percent of women's sports teams in NCAA Divi-sion I were coached by women, leaving six out of ten head coaching roles to men. Fewer than 14 percent of those women's teams were coached by women of color.[9] As professionals in this arena, it is our duty to support and promote participation by members of underrepresented populations. We should be appalled at the inequities and seek means to contribute to a more equitable playing field (literally). The more diverse our coaching cadre, the more likely we are to be able to reach all athletes and prioritize their wellness.

Many people make the mistake of conflating gender identity, gender pre-sentation, and sexual orientation; however, they are separate entities. Making assumptions about a person's sexual orientation based on their gender iden-tity or gender expression is harmful. There are a variety of actions a coach can take to support an inclusive environment in relation to sexual orientation. Such behaviors should be demonstrated by coaches of all genders working with athletes of all genders. Some of the ideas that were suggested for building racial inclusion may be adapted to apply to sexual orientation, such as seeking out and eliminating hidden personal biases, educating yourself, listening to and appreciating the experiences of others, and avoiding tokenizing individu-als. Keep in mind that all types of oppression are different, yet you may find helpful crossover in potential efforts you invest to help minimize harm.

The actions you take to support members of the queer community will help athletes who are comfortable with their queer identities, those who may be closeted or currently unaware of their sexual orientation, and others who have the opportunity to become allies. Coaches may be most successful in assuming that even with a team of athletes who appear and claim to be cisgender and heterosexual, that may not be the case now or indefinitely. If nothing else, athletes need to know from experience that the environment you have created is safe and supportive before they feel comfortable coming out or even participating in the sport. Regardless of your identity and education on topics of sexuality, remember that lived experiences around sexual orientation are unique to each athlete and prioritize the sensitivity and importance of such topics.

Building an inclusive program culture involves both explicit and implicit messaging. To set the stage for supporting all athletes' wellness, it is important to directly acknowledge (in your own beliefs as well as externally) that identities are fluid and may change throughout the season. Provide a space that allows athletes as much or as little room to share their sexual orientation as they would like. As you establish a culture that embraces all sexualities, be aware of what you are subconsciously communicating as well. It may require significant effort on your part to eliminate heteronormative comments in casual conversations. Steer clear of asking questions about, or even playfully assigning, romantic interest to platonic relationships (for example, asking "Is that your *boyfriend*?!" when referring to a friend or someone in the stands). Ensure that topics such as marriage (including those between athletes' parents) are approached inclusively—not strictly as heterosexual. Serve as a role model and guide everyone in the program to minimize further suppression or feelings of isolation for athletes. Such efforts do not assume that all of your athletes will identify as queer, but it creates an environment where all are welcomed and supported. The impact you have on their emotional and social wellness, in particular, may be staggering. Additionally, recognize that there may be specific challenges associated with the intersection of sexual orientation with other aspects of identity. For instance, Black, queer, trans women face significantly increased rates of hate violence.[10]

GENDER AND LGBTQ2+ PERSPECTIVE ON *WINNING WELL*

Linda McLellan

Linda McLellan is a five-time world champion in master's-level games as a member of Team USA, and she competed on one of the first women's professional volleyball teams in the country. She achieved these accolades amid massive equality battles related to Title IX at a time when women were ostracized from the world of sports. Linda was inspired by the coaches who invested in her wellness and following their footsteps as a coach, ensured inclusive environments for all.

Being a child of the sixties and seventies, I experienced some of the most significant and historic eras of change for women. I recall, as a small child, having physical abilities that others struggled with. I wouldn't realize what a gift I had until many years later. As a tomboy, I played every sport boys did and struggled to understand what difference gender made in playing. In fact, my strangest struggle was when I was eleven and not allowed to play Little League baseball even though I was as good as, if not better than, boys at that age. I have never forgotten the ridiculous excuse about requiring players to wear a cup and because I didn't need one, I wasn't allowed the opportunity. When I asked why, I was told it was because it was a rule.

I was a tall, athletically gifted child aspiring to be a roller derby queen since that was the only activity that I was ever exposed to for girls outside of ballet in *The Nutcracker*. Then in middle school, my amazing PE teacher/coach (the first strong-willed, empowered woman I had met besides my mother) introduced me to a variety of physical activities and athletic opportunities. Little did she know, she changed my path forever. I recall her telling me that I should aspire to be a college athlete, despite never hearing anything about women's athletics at the collegiate level. The tables began to turn and for the first time in my life, I felt how setting a goal could be inspiring. Then, Title IX, the landmark federal civil rights law, was passed as a part of the Education Amendments of 1972. This law required gender equality in all aspects of education, including athletics. It wasn't until much later that I understood the value of the women trailblazers who started a rebellion in demanding equal rights, making it possible for me to live authentically.

My high school Girls Athletic Association (GAA) club sports program began to demand the equality that I had longed for. We went from playing our inner squad basketball games with numbered pennies in the cafeteria to expecting the gymnasium and everything that the boys' team had. The feathers of my small community were ruffled, and I felt proudly responsible. To top it off, my friend and I tried out for the boys' team the next year since the girls' team hadn't progressed from the GAA club sport. To my surprise, the boys' coach stormed out of the gym, threatening to quit if girls were going to play on his team. The very next day we had a new coach, uniforms, gym time, and a game schedule.

I do believe my life changed on that day. All that conflict as a young athletic child was now vindicated. My final years of high school offered me semiequal opportunities to participate in a variety of sports, and I did. It was my escape. It provided an environment that supported me holistically and it gave me the power of a purpose that I excelled in.

Upon graduation, I took that rebellion to a whole new level. I went to college, where I escaped the limitations of a small town and enrolled in every athletic activity possible. There I met my second most influential coach in my life. He helped the college navigate the new laws for women athletes and the hiring of coaches for women's sports in order to be in compliance. At first, I thought it was because he had a daughter himself and wanted the same opportunities for her. Later, I realized it was because he had an innate belief that all people deserve equal opportunities to be their true selves. This characteristic fueled his tremendous gift for teaching and coaching each individual person as a human first. He empowered me as a strong woman with a voice and the heart to persevere through any obstacle.

My self-esteem exploded. I would go on to a university with an athletic scholarship playing three sports and excelling through the impact of several quality coaches that continued to challenge me to flourish and share my gift. This empowering reward was priceless.

Finally, I graduated, thinking my athletic life was coming to an end. However, to my surprise, the doors began to open. Professional sports, international-level teams, and opportunities continued to present themselves in my life at every turn. I found myself walking through every door, never looking back. I became a teacher and a coach for the next thirty-five years, motivated to influence the lives of others in the same ways I was. While I was inspired to make an impact on equity, I was driven to empower an athlete towards personal strength before athletic prowess, knowing that nothing was more powerful or longer lasting than what I gained from my mentors.

Through those thirty-five years, I have endured many challenges that required Title IX to be enforced. We are a long way from 100 percent equity, and the fight continues. My students and athletes don't realize how far we have come and often take for granted how good they have it. I have watched fathers fight for their daughters, schools fight for programs, and people demand equality for all genders. I doubt in my lifetime that I will see equity as it should be, but never will a day pass that I won't be fighting for it on a human level. It is essential that we all strive to create environments that embrace all competitors.

Kaig Lightner

Kaig Lightner runs the Portland Community Football Club, where his goal is to provide high-quality, affordable soccer to low-income, migrant, and refugee kids. The club maintains an open acceptance policy of LGBTQ2+ individuals. Kaig identifies as a trans man who came out to his team in a public manner, and his courage went viral worldwide. Taking into consideration all factors that contribute to athlete wellness, he works tirelessly to promote inclusion in sports.

The intersection of sports and gender is incredibly rigid. How sports are organized and categorized bring out an exponential level of rigidity of the gender binary. Trans women participating in sports is when all sorts of people get their hackles up because it's going against patriarchy. It's slapping everyone in the face who believes that men are superior. It really makes them uncomfortable.

What drives me crazy is the fact that people, more often than not, are just trying to find a solution. Are we going to accept trans people in sports or not? Are we going to accept trans women participating against cisgender women or not? And it's not that simple. It's gonna take so much more conversation. It's specific to the sport, it's specific to the athlete, it's specific to the scenario. It has to be something that is looked at holistically and individually and not as a just a new rule that applies to everybody.

I have had some lived experience with that with the soccer club because all the teams are coed. I didn't set out to make it that way. It just happened because we had gaps in rosters and we needed to fill them in. Kids would join the club, and we would just put them all together. It's worked out great. It's provided a lot of opportunity for conversations with kids, particularly for the boys. They've recognized that girls are good at soccer, and it's inspired some of them to work harder. It's brought to light a lot of recognition of the stereotypes that they were holding on to. As the club has continued and the same kids are continuing on with one another, that's become less and less of an issue. They aren't questioning it as much as they used to. The teams compete against teams of all boys typically. Some of this is cultural with the athletes we serve. Often, they come from cultures where girls are not encouraged to play. Parents are not available for childcare, the girls are the next ones in line . . . there are a lot of reasons girls are not as available to play as the boys. The teams that we play against are also from those same cultures, so we see a lot of coed teams.

I am currently coaching our U15 coed team, which at that age, most coaches would be appalled at the idea of a coed group. I always wonder about their hesitancy. We had a game against an all-girls U16 team, so I posted something in our team chat about who we were going to play and it sparked a great conversation in the group. If this were an all-boys high school team, those kinds of conversations most likely wouldn't happen. We wouldn't be in that fertile ground to discuss those things and have those dialogues. In our club, there have just been a lot of scenarios where kids have been able to question the idea of gender in sports.

I didn't necessarily intend to come out so publicly, but I'm glad it worked out the way it did. The reason that it got recorded is that I wanted a historical artifact for myself because it was the first time I had come out to a group of kids that I was coaching. I had come out to lots of other people, but that was a monumental moment. I wanted to be able to share it with parents and any kids that weren't there, so that's why it got put on Facebook. I was naive and thought nobody is going to care about it, but it got picked up by *Out Sports* first, then *Huffington Post*, and then after that happened, it just exploded. It was definitely not my intent, but it is not something that I'm afraid of sharing.

When that happened, we were having a whole new growth in our club and we had a whole new group of families that had just come in. That group of families—all Latino families—were the first people to come to me in person and say, "We love you. We are so glad you did that. We're basically in this together. We understand that you are an oppressed person in some way, and we understand oppression." That was the general message I was getting from them. We were in it together. That was surprising to me. I just thought it was maybe going to be a difficult culture to find inroads, and it has been nothing but positive and nothing but amazing. So that, in and of itself, creates inclusion and connection in the environment.

One of the athletes, Junior, who was a six-year-old at the time, watched that video. A couple years later, he started to express gender fluidity in a really great way. He's been super confident in it and it has also cascaded down to his school. There is a kid in his class who was assigned female at birth and presents and wants to be referred to as a boy and is getting picked on. He was having all the things happen that happen to kids, and Junior basically stepped in and said, "Hey, you're okay. My coach is a transgender (in Junior's words). Nothing is wrong with you." He used my particular story and my relationship with him. Junior understood I'm not a scary person, not a disgusting person. I'm somebody who appreciates him, knows him, loves him, and knows soccer, and connects with him. In his eyes that means, "Great, you used to be a girl and now you're a boy? Okay, anybody can do that." He basically stopped this kid from being bullied anymore in school. For me, that is how athletes have been impacted on a personal level, and it's pretty cool.

Another example: I was sitting in the stands next to a parent who was holding his seven-year-old son on his lap. The little boy said, "Coach, I heard that you were supposed to be a girl." I looked at his dad, who just kind of shrugged, laughed, and didn't say anything. He didn't stop the conversation from happening, which was great. I feel like so many parents will jump in saying, "No, no, no, that's not appropriate; don't say that." But this parent let the dialogue happen. The kid and I proceeded to have a very appropriate seven-year-old conversation. I asked him, "What do you mean by 'supposed to be'?" and he replied that he didn't really know, but that Junior had told him about me. So I said, "Well, I used to be a girl and now I look like this." And he simply stated, "Okay!" and got off his dad's lap and just ran off. Like, I just answered all of his questions. Those kinds of conversations for kids that are growing up in the world of sports are so important. Hopefully that planted a little bit of a seed for that seven-year-old that things aren't always as they seem.

For Junior, who I have a much deeper relationship with, he's getting to understand the idea that you can be who you want to be. You can present yourself however you want to present yourself. He's stepping into his gender expression and gender identity, and who knows what it is. He's just stepping into it, going with what feels good to him. And he's a phenomenal soccer player. You can have both. When I think about being as out as I am and being a voice (whatever that means) of trans people, that's why it's important to me.

That was the whole reason for me to be so out in the club and not have it be a club that is entirely focused on LGBTQ+. All aspects of identity are a part of it. It allows us to foster an environment where you're an immigrant kid, you're a kid who grew up in a refugee camp, you're a queer kid, you're a trans kid, you're a white, low-income kid . . . everyone belongs. It's all a part of the large sphere of the human experience, and we just get to come together and play soccer together. It doesn't need to be so siloed. It allows kids to just be themselves and express themselves in whatever way feels good to them. I didn't know what was going to happen when that video went viral. I didn't know how it was going to impact the kids in the club, but I'm seeing it now start to play out. It's pretty amazing and unique.

Being myself has allowed everyone in the club to be themselves. Successful coaches know that if you get down to an appropriate personal level with your players, they want to work hard for you. There is strength in those connections and as a result, there is power in the coaching role. That power can be used in a positive way to include all athletes and support them holistically.

Melissa Mulick

Melissa Mulick grew up playing every sport she had access to, seeking a community in which she could be herself. As someone who spent her first twenty-four years hiding and ashamed of her sexual orientation, Melissa has reflected back on her experiences, and now, as a volleyball coach, consciously provides a more inclusive environment for athletes. While she may not have found what she needed in sports for herself in this respect, she has changed the trajectory and positively impacted countless others' wellness as a result.

Growing up in a small town where my closeted lesbian identity caused me much anxiety, sports were my safe haven. The volleyball court provided an energetic outlet, and a shared passion for the sport bonded me to my teammates. I struggled a lot with internalized homophobia and self-hatred throughout adolescence and wasn't able to come out as a lesbian until my midtwenties. Even then, it took about three years of therapy and introspective work to come to a place where I was accepting of my sexuality. In hindsight, I believe that because my sports teams felt so supportive and like the safest environments I knew, had they been less heteronormative I may have been able to come out a decade earlier than I did. I always felt pressure that in order to fit in with my teammates and coaches, I had to be straight. I look back and one of the things I dream of is having had a gay coach. A gay coach who was out and managing to live a successful life?! That would have been an absolute game changer for me and my sense of self-worth!

Knowing that my former coaches were more than likely straight, having a straight coach who explicitly communicated that they would understand and accept me even if I went to prom with a girl would have had a massive impact. When nothing was said and only heteronormative comments were made, I assumed that there was something wrong with me that needed to be fixed. Ultimately, silence from my straight coaches further supported my collection of data that I internalized as proof of my inherent "wrongness."

When I began playing collegiate volleyball, I joined a team of highly feminine-presenting, straight, cis women. It was a well-known thing that at my school, volleyball girls dated basketball guys. Our social lives revolved around planning parties and nights out with the men's basketball team. This was never questioned, and every new class of players seemed to accept it and do their best to perpetuate the pattern. Chitchat during warm-ups and stretching often centered around what outfits people were going to wear out that night, who was dating who, and it was always entirely heteronormative. I never once heard any of my teammates—who had become my chosen college family—ever throw out anything positive or affirming related to a same-sex relationship. I craved validation of my internal (gay) self but felt the need to fit in even more. I pretended to have crushes on basketball boys in order to fit in, but it felt 100 percent wrong 100 percent of the time. I ached for a teammate to acknowledge the existence of queerness and to let me know that I wouldn't lose the love of my team if I came out. It never happened. Over four years my teammates only discussed hetero love and I played along in order to maintain my safety with them.

At the age of twenty-seven, I joined a lesbian softball league and—for the first time in my life—played on a team while I was out. It was freeing in a way that I'd never experienced as a player before. I got to bond with my teammates about our games, during happy hours, and over our shared identity as queer women. It was a level of validation I'd never felt before and one I hope to foster as much as possible for my players. Sports were my safe haven, but there was a whole level of safety that wasn't even accessible to me as a young athlete. I can't do that part of my life over again, but as a coach I work really hard to create a more open environment for my athletes than I was afforded.

Now that I'm out and proud and in my thirteenth year of coaching, I make it a significant point to use inclusive language with my teenage players. Regardless of how they outwardly identify, when dances or dating are a topic of conversation I make sure to explicitly state that I'm excited to hear about anyone's experience of dating boys, girls, nonbinary folks, or how they had fun with their friends if they identify as asexual or aromantic. I always want to make sure that any closeted athlete hears directly from me that even if it's not safe enough for them to be out yet, I support any and all potential identities they may have. I out myself to my players early on in every season so that they don't just see me as their coach, but they get to know me as a whole person—which very much includes my sexual orientation.

APPLICATIONS IN COACH DEVELOPMENT: SUPPORTING INCLUSION, GROWTH, AND PRODUCTIVE CONVERSATION

Systemic oppression is both underidentified and ignored in athletics. Consequently, it is imperative that the people who are leading coaches are aware of the inequities in sport and are dedicated to making a change. Some coaches and programs may be acutely aware of challenges faced by their players, families, and communities, and others are not. The discrepancies in opportunity and bias inherent in standard operations of any given sports program may need to be identified from your fresh, outside perspective. Taking a critical look at the structures, habits, and culture of a sports program is the first step in moving that program toward inclusion.[1] Coach development efforts should be centered around providing quality sports for all, and committing to inclusion as a fundamental principle of our work is a must.

When engaging in inclusion-focused dialogue with coaches authentically, purposefully, and explicitly, the conversations will likely be uncomfortable. Such communication paves the route to increased awareness and the resulting potential growth and progress of both individuals and organizations.[2] Specific to promoting racial inclusion, Brian Gearity and colleagues suggest that "coach developers should remember to explore a coach's knowledge, attitudes, and feelings, how others may feel, and consider actions coaches can take to rectify unearned privileges and embody antiracist practices. It's likely less important that coaches know exactly what to do in every situation than developing a deep understanding of race and WP [white privilege], including racial interpersonal and systemic harm, and acquire an array of practical skills to use in varying contexts to identify and act on these issues."[3]

Suggestions for facilitating brave conversations are rapidly expanding and evolving. It is in the best interest of coach developers to lean on experts to help maintain a repertoire of relevant and effective strategies.[4] Many models encourage participants to choose to stay engaged, experience discomfort, speak their truth respectfully, and expect and accept nonclosure.[5] While the specifics of such recommendations may shift over time, establishing mutual agreements for inclusion discourse is key.

Co-constructing and agreeing to a set of guiding principles for difficult conversations helps set the tone for openness, engagement, and a shared purpose. As you venture into discussions with coaches, keep the overarching goal in mind and be cognizant of the intersectional identities you both bring to the table.[6] Through your modeling and discussion, you can also help coaches to determine their own set of best practices in relation to related conversations with athletes and others.

Notes

1. Ahada McCummings and Caitlin Mance, "USCCE Engagement Event: Community Engagement for Diversified Programming," presented in the United States Center for Coaching Excellence Community Engagement Series, November 19, 2020.

2. Glenn E. Singleton, *Courageous Conversations about Race: A Field Guide for Achieving Equity in Schools*, 2nd ed. (Thousand Oaks, CA: Corwin, 2015).

3. Brian Gearity, Lynett Henderson Metzger, Derrick S. Wong, and Ted Butryn, "Understanding and Acting upon White Privilege in Coaching and Coach Education," in *Coach Education and Development in Sport: Instructional Strategies*, edited by Bettina Callary and Brian Gearity (New York: Routledge, 2020), 253.

4. Sam Killermann and Meg Bolger, *Unlocking the Magic of Facilitation: 11 Key Concepts You Didn't Know You Didn't Know* (Austin, TX: Impetus Books, 2016).

5. Brian Arao and Kristi Clemens, "From Safe Spaces to Brave Spaces: A New Way to Frame Dialogue around Diversity and Social Justice," in *The Art of Effective Facilitation: Reflections from Social Justice Educators*, edited by Lisa Landreman (Sterling, VA: Stylus Publishing, 2013), 135–50; Singleton, *Courageous Conversations about Race*; Gearity, Metzger, Wong, and Butryn, "Understanding and Acting upon White Privilege in Coaching and Coach Education."

6. Singleton, *Courageous Conversations about Race*.

Occupational Wellness

Sport teaches you character, it teaches you to play by the rules, it teaches you to know what it feels like to win and lose—it teaches you about life.

—*Billie Jean King*

WHAT IS OCCUPATIONAL WELLNESS IN THE CONTEXT OF SPORTS?

Occupational wellness is characterized by finding satisfaction and/or purpose in our work. It's about contributing to ourselves, our families, and others. In sports, it involves fostering skills that are applied in the workplace, determining boundaries around the identity of "coach" or "athlete" within the scope of life, and managing the retirement from sports that we all face at some point. For coaches, occupational wellness is a vital component of overall wellness. It greatly impacts potential for success and allows for the opportunity to promote the coaching profession for future generations. Regardless of age or competitive level of play, athletes learn lessons that can influence their occupational wellness throughout their lives.

Coach Sam will tell us if we want to get a job, to get one. He says not to make basketball everything in our life and to focus on other things. He tells us school first and then basketball. Even if our best player doesn't get good grades, he will sit them.

—*Grant, age 15*

WHY DOES OCCUPATIONAL WELLNESS MATTER
IN THE WORLD OF ATHLETICS?

As humans, we want, need, and deserve fulfillment in our work; coaches are no exception. At times, coaching can feel like a thankless profession. It requires a lot of effort and possibly some sacrifice, but it shouldn't take over your entire life. For most coaches, being able to coach is a luxury, and it should feel like a luxury as well. As long as you are coaching, you should be excited about the time you get to spend with athletes. If you have lost that passion or fire, that is concerning—*and* it is also normal. Feeling a little blah about coaching can happen for a variety of reasons, and it doesn't necessarily mean it's time to hang it up. It often simply indicates that your occupational wellness needs a bit of attention.

For athletes who break through the amateur boundary and for those who do not, your commitment to coaching the whole person should include supporting learning and intellectual growth. If you are working with athletes who are in school, that is one of their occupations, and you have the opportunity and responsibility to support their efforts in the classroom. Only 6 percent of high school athletes move on to compete at the college level, and of that small percentage, fewer than 2 percent of them make it to the pros.[1] A solid educational background serves as an excellent support net.

Regardless of the athlete's final destination in sports, most will enter into the working world, and the athletic experience can greatly influence their capacity in career and professional roles. Athletes not only develop dedication, teamwork, a growth mindset, and self-esteem, they are also provided with the opportunity to hone in on their own leadership skills. Those skills and abilities that can be taken into the occupational world are priceless and may be difficult to obtain elsewhere.[2]

While your current investment in building perseverance and cooperation in athletes may play out in the game of life, the short-term gains you see on the field can also be tremendous. The qualities that qualify someone as employee of the month are often the same competencies that describe players of the year. Teams or programs that exhibit excellence regularly demonstrate significant crossover with thriving businesses and organizations. Winning teams are characterized by the same values, attitudes, and behaviors, regardless of their context and industry.[3] Consequently, promoting occupational wellness in athletes is well worth the results you see on the scoreboard and beyond.

I love being an athlete because it has taught me how to have a strong work ethic. An athlete has to work hard for everything, such as learning new skills, competing under pressure, and continuing to push through during the hard times. All of these skills are learned through success and failure. When you fail, you can't give up. You learn and keep trying until you get it right.

Goal setting is essential if you want to achieve success and it is a big part of gymnastics. I tend to set myself goals at the beginning of each week, and I try to get even 2 percent better in that week. All those small improvements build up over time and pay off. Of course, the hard work has to go along with achieving your goals, but if you tell yourself you are going to get something done, you will do it through determination and hard work.

—*Audrey, age 14*

PROBLEM: ALL CAREERS COME TO AN END

In terms of occupational wellness, the problem is not that we see occupational issues creep onto the field or mat, but rather that we don't manage the transition out of sport well. This section addresses that transition alone—the associated difficulties and suggestions for supporting the end of coaching and athletic careers.

In *The Weight of Gold*, a heart-wrenching documentary about the challenges faced by Olympic athletes after the games have ended, Michael Phelps does not mince words about the dire need for emotional support. The movie depicts the all-too-common reality that Olympians face as they struggle to find steady ground mentally and emotionally following their performance on the world stage. Athletes of all genders from all sports share their stories along with Phelps, who explains, "We're human. I don't think I have to say anything else. We're human beings just like everybody else. Yeah, I had won a shit ton of medals. I had a great career. It doesn't matter. I wasn't happy with who I was. I thought of myself as just a swimmer and not a human being. Not a person. No self-love, no self-confidence. . . . It's okay to not be okay."[4]

While the intensity of the Olympic experience is unique, the need for support for all athletes is universal and it is typically undervalued, ignored, and dismissed. Careers end, and athletic careers are no exception to the rule. Whether due to burnout, injury, being cut, or changing interests, everyone ends their playing career at some point. Recognizing the intensity of the transition out of sports is essential for coaches and athletes alike. The end of a career brings numerous challenges, and much like retirement from the workforce, many of us feel ill prepared to wrap things up. There may be scholarships and hopes and dreams on the line or maybe even just the pride of dominating the adult kickball league. Regardless, sports bring us joy, satisfaction, social connection, and a physical outlet, and watching that all come to an end can be extremely difficult.

At the highest levels of athletics, we see tragic and troubling trends among the retired athlete population, including bankruptcy, family struggles, divorce, substance abuse, and depression. With so much of an athlete's life wrapped up in their identity as an athlete, we should be very aware of the difficulties they may face, which may apply at any level of sport.[5] While leagues are doing a better job of providing supports for retiring athletes at the professional and NCAA levels, it is often on coaches at all levels to assist athletes on their way out the door. It is an essential step in promoting the overall wellness of a player, and your compassion at this time may be as important as ever.

Just like the athletes, your career as a coach will come to an end at some point, and in a similar vein, it is likely that a good portion of your identity may be entangled in your coaching. Coaches leave the field frequently, which is both unfortunate and understandable. Challenges may arise that do not feel worth your while and you may exit on good terms for healthy reasons; for example, some coaches leave to "get their lives back" or to take care of themselves or their families. Coaching should be something that you do; it should not encompass all that you are. If you can stay in the game while prioritizing your wellness and the things that are most valuable to you, great. If not, it may be time for a break, and that break may or may not need to be permanent.

Regardless of the circumstances in which a coach leaves the profession, being vulnerable and honest about happiness, satisfaction, and well-being may be extremely difficult. Finding others who can understand the intensity of the moment, show support, and empathize is a must. Regardless of the level at which you coach, your win-loss record, and the number of years you've spent in the field, the experience likely had a powerful impact on you. As a result, leaving will likely have its challenges. If you can be honest with athletes about why you are leaving, there is a lot they might be able to learn about work-life balance, keeping things in perspective, and valuing your own personal wellness. At some point, they too will be at the end of their career (or at some sort of a break), and how you take care of yourself, the professionalism you demonstrate, and the respect you give to others will be remembered for many years to come. Most importantly, take care of *yourself* as you leave—it can be a very tough decision to make and a difficult transition to manage.

A NOTE ON FEASIBILITY AS IT RELATES TO OCCUPATIONAL WELLNESS

In relation to maximizing occupational wellness, a few barriers that you may encounter include, but are not limited to, the following:

- Perspectives of the roles and associated values of an occupation vary greatly.
- Cultural and familial differences exist related to academic expectations and career preparation priorities.
- The identity of "athlete" may encompass a variety of intensities, priorities, and understandings. This may be very different from your own definition.

While this list is not exhaustive, taking the time to acknowledge potential barriers to wellness is imperative.

Occupational wellness in sports supports athletes in feeling inspired and fulfilled at work or in school, promotes the coaching profession and career-applicable skills that can be learned through sport, recognizes "athlete" as a partial identity, and supports each person's journey through sports and beyond.

WHERE ARE YOU NOW?

1. How do you feel about your current occupational wellness?
2. How do you feel about the occupational wellness of the athletes you coach?
3. How much of a priority is it for you to support your athletes' occupational wellness?
4. How well-informed and prepared do you feel to help maximize occupational wellness in the athletes you coach?
5. How do your personal and coaching practices support or detract from your athletes' occupational wellness?

TIPS FOR SUPPORTING YOUR OWN OCCUPATIONAL WELLNESS

It would not be out of the ordinary for you to leave practice one day think-ing you have the best job in the world and leave the very next day wondering why on earth you do this work at all. Coaching is intense *and* it should feel good. In relation to your occupational wellness, give yourself the chance to honestly reflect on your feelings and satisfaction in this role. As a result of that reflection, find a way to enjoy the ride, embrace the challenges, and maintain boundaries that promote your health and happiness. Below are some sugges-tions for making the most of this profession and modeling that for athletes:

- Evaluate your wellness in all dimensions to help you clarify the source of a problem when one exists. It may be something directly related to coaching and it may not.
- Surround yourself with positive influences and people who find the same type of enjoyment in the work as you do. A staff and coaching support system that shares your values and strives for positive experiences has the potential to boost your occupational wellness significantly.
- Set boundaries around the amount of time and energy you are willing to dedicate to the work as it relates to the pay (or lack thereof). Do what feels appropriate to you and enriches your life.
- Embrace your identity outside of sports. Coaching may be your passion and what you consider to be your greatest work, but you are still a human outside of the work.
- Focus on and maximize the parts of the job that you enjoy most.
- Consider making even a slight adjustment to bring enthusiasm and energy back to your work if things are feeling a bit dull.
- Expand your knowledge and skills to help reignite your flame with the profession.
- Laugh with your athletes and your fellow coaches! Celebrate the good times, regardless of how small they may seem. Sports are not a matter of life or death—keep things in perspective.

TIPS FOR SUPPORTING ATHLETES' OCCUPATIONAL WELLNESS

Demonstrating a healthy relationship with your work inspires occupational wellness in athletes. The following tips for modeling occupational wellness are provided along with a handful of other suggestions:

- Establish and maintain work boundaries as a coach, and communicate those boundaries to players and parents. You can always be available to athletes and families in case of an emergency, but determine your preferred schedule and ensure your actions consistently reinforce those boundaries; for example, don't e-mail players in the middle of the night because you happen to be watching film. If you have decided that Sundays are a day that you want to invest in your family, don't reach out to players or parents about items that can wait until the beginning of the week. Balance for you *and* your athletes is essential.

- Check your own privilege and biases as they relate to work, the purpose of a career, and what kind of skills you consider to be work related.

- Explicitly teach and discuss work-related skills with players.[6] The odds that they will magically comprehend that a drill is reinforcing a specific work-related skill on their own are slim to none. Like any life skill you emphasize with players, you need to name the skill, practice it, and help players to connect it to their work in the classroom or current/future profession, and beyond.

- Whether you coach in a school setting or not, support academic and career efforts. Touch base with athletes individually to stay up to date on their school experience. Be informed of stressful times throughout the school year and important events such as standardized testing periods, finals weeks, and the beginning and end of each term. Being aware of players' stress may prove extremely helpful for you and for them.

- Celebrate academic and career successes with individual players and/or the entire team. Be aware of the varying experiences athletes may have had in school or work and avoid publicly reinforcing the struggles of some and triumphs of others, as this may be a pattern that has existed for many years for certain individuals. Keep individual grades confidential and do your best to support effort, improvement, resilience, and open-mindedness.

- Promote the coaching profession itself and be open to discussing some of the challenges as well. Through your day-to-day actions and conveyance of your love for the work, you can inspire the next generation of coaches.

- While promoting empathy for officials, administrators, and other sport or game employees, remain open to connecting players with a deeper understanding of those occupations. Value the role of everyone who makes playing the game possible, and foster players' interests in those roles through various efforts. For example, bring in an official as a guest speaker; write team thank-you notes to custodians, ticket salespeople, scorebook keepers, or clock operators; or set up opportunities for players to volunteer at other sport or youth events. Such experiences can be great team-building activities as well.

- Encourage or offer athletes an opportunity to coach and/or officiate. If you run camps or events for younger athletes, involve older players in the process. Not only does teaching others allow them to engage in the deepest kind of learning,[7] it may inspire an interest in contributing to the game for life.

- Help athletes to value their whole identity as individuals, both in and out of sport. Even for athletes at the highest levels of the game, it is essential that they know they are more than "just an athlete." While coaches tend to be inspired by the most dedicated competitors and seek a high level of commitment, remember the importance of maintaining balance.

- Discuss your empathy around injuries, burnout, and careers coming to an end. Be proactive about this so that players know about their support net prior to an issue. Demonstrate empathy for opponents and others in the sporting world going through those challenges and use examples, as appropriate, to teach players to show respect and support for others. Carefully communicate around these topics to avoid conveying that the end of sport is the end of life, while simultaneously recognizing the difficulty. Such discussions provide a great reminder to enjoy the game while you are a part of it.

APPLICATIONS IN COACH DEVELOPMENT:
LEVERAGING COACH WELLNESS AND
FULFILLMENT

Coaches, much like athletes, aim for optimal performance, and as a result, striving for success in all dimensions of wellness is vital.[1] Allowing the wheels to fall off in any one dimension of wellness disrupts the entire wellness process and coaching experience. The efforts that you make as a coach developer to support and enhance coaches' wellness are not only noble, they have the potential to boost coaches' developmental capacity. High-level learning, striving for excellence, and reflectively seeking new challenges are all demanding tasks that are most confidently managed when someone feels (and is) on top of their game. Because that level of participation is what coach development asks of coaches, it is in your best interest to leverage wellness in your favor. Coaches will be healthier, happier, and more fulfilled, and your collaboration will have the potential to reach incredible heights.

As one of the most connected and informed members of a coach's support system, you may be the most aptly positioned to ensure they prioritize their own personal wellness amid the challenges of coaching. Because coaches are aware of your mutual interest in their development, they may be more open to your expressing concern for their wellness than they would someone who is less invested in their performance as a coach.[2] In this same vein, you may also have a considerable amount of influence in relation to assessing and encouraging enjoyment in their work. If they are questioning their desire to stay in the profession, you can be a trusted confidant who does not judge them, while continuing to help them succeed in the moment. Due to the nature of your role, coaches can rest assured that you care about their coaching. When you pair that with concern for them as people, you may be able to greatly impact their capacity for fulfillment both personally and professionally.

Notes

1. United States Olympic and Paralympic Committee, Quality Coaching Framework (2020), https://www.teamusa.org/About-the-USOPC/Programs/Coaching-Education/Quality-Coaching-Framework.

2. François Rodrigue and Pierre Trudel, "A 'Personal Learning Coach' for High-Performance Coaches," In *Coach Education and Development in Sport: Instructional Strategies*, edited by Bettina Callary and Brian Gearity (New York: Routledge, 2020), 141–53.

STORIES OF *WINNING WELL* IN OCCUPATIONAL WELLNESS

Brittney (Anderson) Martin

Throughout her playing days, Brittney (Anderson) Martin was well known for her work ethic and unparalleled love of basketball. For those who were lucky enough to play with Britt and coach her, she was an ideal teammate. What she gained in sports is demonstrated regularly in her current career.

Britt learned lessons from her coach that directly impact how she connects with patients in her occupation as a physical therapist.

I tore my ACL the summer going into my sophomore year in college. I had two doctors and two athletic trainers look at my knee and all of them said I was fine, so I kept playing and training to get ready for preseason. When open gyms started in September, my knee still didn't feel right, but it didn't hurt. I had the school doctor at my university look at it and we finally discovered it was torn. I made the decision to brace it and play the season with it torn, and then had surgery once the season ended. I worked hard, rehabbing and training, to get back for my junior year. Then, that December before Christmas break, I tore my meniscus in the same knee. Again, I decided to play through it and have a second surgery after the season was over.

There was nothing about this situation that was ideal to me, but I did the best I could to make the most of the challenges I faced. I absolutely love playing basketball. I wanted more than anything to be able to continue to play and to finish out my college career on a good note. While I had never been a player who needed any extra attention or help from a coach, in retrospect, everything my coach did for me was amazing. She helped me to both physically and emotionally recover and thrive given the circumstances. Had Coach not been there and cared the way she did, I have no idea how I would have managed my struggles and disappointment.

In terms of my physical wellness, it was clear that my full recovery was Coach's top priority. She understood the recovery process following both surgeries. She didn't make me feel pressured to get back on the court ahead of pace. She made sure I was completing my rehab every day, both before and after surgery. When I had been cleared to return, she eased me into practices, even though I was fully cleared by the doctor, to help me regain confidence. She would talk with the trainers to make sure I was truly okay and not hiding other injuries.

Coach and I talked a lot about my knee and how I was feeling, but even when we weren't talking about it, she was paying attention, and it was obvious that she cared. When I was playing with my ACL torn, I never asked for a day off or any kind of special treatment. But I remember there was one day where I felt like I just needed a break, and when I walked into practice that day, she already had plans to sit me out and run the clock for practice while I iced. She was aware enough to recognize it without me having to say anything.

In addition to ensuring that I was physically okay, Coach was also very supportive emotionally. Before finding out my ACL was torn, I went to the school doctor's office alone because I truly did not think I was injured that badly. I was shocked and very upset after finding out I had a potentially career-ending injury. Coach drove over an hour to meet me. She comforted me and talked me through my options because my family was not able to be there. She even called my parents and gave them more information than I could at the time. She then came to all future appointments with me and was there for my MRIs. When I was unable to participate in traditional preseason workouts, she let me help her create the workouts/training schedule to make me still feel like I was a part of the team. She would always check in on me because she understood the emotional toll of playing through and recovering from injuries (having torn her ACL back when she was playing as well).

I feel like if I did not have a coach that understood like she did, I might not have been able to return to sport, or I could have possibly returned too soon, which might have led to even more injuries. Coach's support for me in both a physical sense as well as an emotional sense changed my life. I could not have asked for more out of a coach. She was definitely there for me in my hardest times, and it was clear that she cared about me as a person, not just a player.

The way that Coach helped support me has greatly influenced my current professional philosophy and occupational success. As a physical therapist, I 100 percent focus on both the physical and emotional aspects of injuries with all my patients. I've been through it and understand how hard it can be, so I want to offer them support to help them regain their quality of life in the safest way possible.

Jeff Zerba

Jeff Zerba is well respected within the wrestling community for the success he has experienced as a coach while surmounting daunting challenges. During his own prep career, he sustained a life-altering injury, and he credits what he learned through athletics with helping him to thrive professionally. Zerba's coaching philosophy is centered around teaching athletes life skills and setting them up to prosper in any career.

In grade school and middle school, I participated in all sports and eventually earned varsity letters in wrestling, football, and cross country. When I started wrestling, however, I excelled. I was able to try both Grecco-Roman and freestyle and learned it was my sport.

Through wrestling, I learned to set goals, and in eighth grade, I set a goal to be a state champion. In high school I wasn't the greatest, but I worked really hard. By my junior year I had grown quite a bit and had really high expectations for the season. I worked out three times a day and it paid off. I ended up being a three-time district champion and won a couple state titles during that time. I learned a lot from my high school coach. He wasn't the best technically, but he was very organized and taught us a lot about work ethic. He was always there and if he wanted us to go to a tournament, he would go too—he wouldn't just send us with a club coach. As a wrestling coach, he walked his talk.

Wrestling definitely taught me how to work hard. I love that it is an individual sport. I like that what you put into it, you get out of it. Even though we had common team goals, we had individual goals too. Wrestling is cool that way.

I got hurt my junior year in a freestyle match. The guy I was wrestling went to throw me, and I landed on the back of my neck. My vertebrae were dislocated, and as a result of the injury to my spinal cord, I became a quadriplegic. It was just a bad situation. I had thrown that move and been thrown in that move a hundred times; it just didn't go well that one time. I try to tell people that all the time, and when it happened, I wanted to make sure everyone knew that. I reached out to the guy I had been wrestling to make sure he knew it was just a bad thing that happened, and that I didn't blame him for it. We hadn't really been friends previously, but we actually got a little bit closer because of the freak accident.

At this point, I am paralyzed from my chest down and am in a wheelchair. I have some use of my arms, and thankfully, I don't have to be in an electric wheelchair, like most quadriplegic people. I have full use of my biceps and about 5 percent of my triceps. I can move my hands but not my fingers. I don't have a lot of balance. I can feel parts of my body, which is great because a lot of people in my position cannot. When I first got hurt, I had the unrealistic goal of walking again. I thought I could just beat this injury. I went to a spinal cord rehab unit at Craig Hospital in Colorado, and I discovered in rehab that wasn't going to happen.

Midway through rehab, I started to get more function back in general, and my main goal was to set myself up to be independent. I had enough triceps to lift myself out of my chair. I wanted to be able to do most things on my own without having to use too many different devices. I definitely needed my wheelchair and accessibility to get up and down stairs and in and out of spaces. As I was going through rehab, it was clear that wrestling had helped me a lot. It taught me to be patient, goal oriented, and to adapt to my new lifestyle.

After I won my first state championship, my dream to earn a full-ride college scholarship was set in motion. Because of my injury, I realized it wasn't going to happen, but I was active in choir, leadership, and other extracurriculars. So I was able to get three-quarters of my school paid through scholarships. I finished my senior year and helped out with the team that season. My self-esteem was really low. I was very critical of how I looked, what people thought of me, and the way people treated me because of what happened and who I had become. I just wasn't the same type of person, and that was pretty difficult. I was so worried about being in a wheelchair.

Originally, I wanted to go to the Air Force Academy to wrestle. I thought I would find an occupation where I could fly planes, but the injury stopped me from being able to do that, so I ended up going to Oregon State University instead. The biggest challenge was learning how to be in a wheelchair and navigate life. Wrestling, again, helped me to persevere. Being an athlete taught me how to work hard and to be resilient. I had learned to be able to focus on things. In school, I was able to focus on keeping my grades up and being independent. Two years into college, I was able to do pretty much everything on my own except tie my shoes and get up stairs.

I connected with the wrestling coach on campus and worked with the team for five years. I went to practice every day and I pretty much ran the practices. I learned how to coach from a wheelchair and was debating careers I could do from my chair. I thought I would be a great wrestling coach, so I changed my major to health education and human performance. My health teacher in high school was one of my role models, so I followed in his footsteps.

I was turned down for multiple coaching jobs because I was in a wheelchair, and people didn't know how I would coach from my chair. Eventually, I was given a chance and landed the same coaching job I have today. It doesn't take kids a long time to realize I know what I am doing. Obviously, I'm not on the mat showing them anything, but my communication skills are good. Even though I cannot show the technique, I verbalize the technique and use my kids to show the technique for me.

I emulate what my coach taught me in relation to work ethic. My athletes get how hard I work, and that builds their awareness of how hard they are capable of working. I emphasize goal setting, and my athletes know that it's more about the process and hard work than about the outcome. I believe we have learned a ton by wrestling and, in many cases, losing to some of the best wrestling teams in the state.

The higher the expectations I have for athletes, the more insight that gives them into what they are capable of, especially since I am in a wheelchair. I like that I can demonstrate work ethic and how to power through adversity. With everything that I have been through, athletes see how those skills have benefited me. People always ask me, "How do you coach even though this horrific thing has happened to you?" The thing that happened to me was really just a flukey deal, and because of what I learned in wrestling, I am able to persevere and can teach athletes some of those same lessons.

Maybe an athlete isn't going to be a state champion, but they can see how the goal-setting process and their own high expectations lead to success. They learn to value their work ethic and efforts on and off the mat. They can apply everything they learn in wrestling to other aspects of life, like education and careers. What I learned in wrestling has made me who I am today, and I am grateful for the opportunity to help athletes set themselves up for success later in life as well.

Financial Wellness

Accessibility allows us to tap into everyone's potential.

—*Debra Ruh*

WHAT IS FINANCIAL WELLNESS IN THE CONTEXT OF SPORTS?

Financial wellness is about feeling safe and secure. It is not about keeping up with the Joneses, winning the lottery, or selling your soul for financial gain, but being in a place financially that results in limited or manageable stress. Financial comfort and safety can mean a variety of things to different people.

The pay-to-play model has undoubtedly changed the face of sports culture. Those activities that started as games among friends and strangers in a back-yard, playground, or park have become costly, time-intensive investments on the part of sport families. Currently, sports are not available to all—inequities abound! Thankfully, there are efforts to eliminate such barriers and shift the culture, because our current reality leaves much to be desired.[1]

One of the primary goals of current and future initiatives within sports is to increase accessibility. Factors that impact access include, but are not limited to, participation fees, purchasing and caring for uniforms and equipment, and maintaining proper exercise nutrition. Practice times and locations may conflict with family commitments, jobs, and travel to the track, pool, field, ice, or court. There are numerous considerations, and there will always be barriers for certain individuals and groups until we make major changes in our society. As coaches, we need to be aware of the realities of each athlete's experience and work to minimize barriers. A commitment to improving access to quality sports experiences for all is essential.

WHY DOES FINANCIAL WELLNESS MATTER IN THE WORLD OF ATHLETICS?

Doing your part in minimizing inequities, increasing awareness around such issues, and modeling relatable money management strategies to the best of your ability all play a role in the financial wellness you can help build in athletes. Taking care of yourself financially and being open to appropriate conversations about finances may be helpful. While it may not be something that comes to mind midpractice, financial wellness has the potential to impact performance on a variety of levels.

Coming at this from a strictly performance-based approach, financial wellness is not to be overlooked. You may be missing out on working with the best athletes in your town or city because of financial barriers. In addition, when you think of the stress that can be caused by financial strife, it is not hard to imagine that athletes (and their families) struggle through the daily grind. With that kind of stress, how in the world do you expect athletes to perform at the top of their game? You may not be able to fix their issues, but it is possible to provide tools to help build and promote financial capacity so that people don't feel quite as helpless and trapped. If financial literacy were something we all learned and if quality sports programs were available to all athletes, the strength of our programs and teams would improve across the board. Your efforts in this area may come up with bigger benefits than you think, even in terms of wins and losses.

Our coach tells us not to be afraid to ask our parents questions, like how much different things cost, how much they pay for certain bills, or how much things will cost for us in the future. Coach teaches us how to be responsible in our lives.

—*Cameron, age 14*

PROBLEM: WHEN DID SPORTS BECOME ELITIST?!

On a national level, the Aspen Institute has exposed numerous concerning trends in the world of sports. The institute's *State of Play* report identifies a variety of struggles as well as opportunities for improvement. When we take a closer look at sports culture in particular, we see an increase in barriers to participation for athletes coming from lower-income households. With an average annual cost of $693 per child, per sport, we have created a massive issue.[2]

There are health impacts associated with financial wellness. Young people are being deprived of valuable physical activity in their day. Discrepancy in opportunities goes well beyond the playing field. This is a wellness issue—something that impacts athletes on a holistic level and demands our attention. According to Dave Egner, "We have a health crisis in our society, and access to sport can address that. And if we can expand access to free-play opportunities, we can expand the creativity and problem-solving skills of the next generation. This is about civilization and developing leaders moving forward. It's much bigger than I thought it was."[3]

The sports world desperately needs our help and attention in this area right now. While it may feel uncomfortable or challenging to examine, address, and promote financial wellness through sports, we owe it to ourselves and all athletes to do so. When we make improvements to the system that benefit our most disenfranchised, we build a better system, one that is stronger for everyone involved. In terms of wellness in sport, there are very few areas with the glaring inequities we see when we really dive into financial wellness.

A NOTE ON FEASIBILITY AS IT RELATES TO FINANCIAL WELLNESS

In relation to maximizing financial wellness, a few barriers that you may encounter include, but are not limited to, the following:

- There is great variety in the ways that families discuss and relate to money.
- There is significant variability in financial literacy among us as a result of many societal issues.
- The debate and potential plans for paying collegiate athletes continues, and it may have a significant impact on athletes and the way in which we all approach sports from a financial perspective.

While this list is not exhaustive, taking the time to acknowledge potential barriers to wellness is imperative.

Financial wellness in sports promotes financial literacy to help athletes feel stable financially and strives to make sports accessible to everyone.

WHERE ARE YOU NOW?

1. How do you feel about your current financial wellness?
2. How do you feel about the financial wellness of the athletes you coach?
3. How much of a priority is it for you to support your athletes' financial wellness?
4. How well-informed and prepared do you feel to help maximize financial wellness in the athletes you coach?
5. How do your personal and coaching practices support or detract from your athletes' financial wellness?

TIPS FOR SUPPORTING YOUR OWN FINANCIAL WELLNESS

Financial wellness can impact health and happiness significantly. Because of that aspect alone, it deserves our attention, for both you and athletes. The following are a few considerations for you around financial wellness:

- Build your own financial intelligence and budget appropriately for your life. The goal is to feel secure and minimize stressors in this arena, which may look different for you in comparison to anyone else. Financial pressures to portray a particular image, conform to specific purchasing, or act in certain ways around money are very prevalent for some. Be cognizant of those pressures and take care of yourself within your means.
- Remember that it is not your responsibility to personally fund your entire program. Sharing with athletes or giving back to the program at a reasonable level (through a camp, for example) can be a nice way to show your love for the program, but it isn't necessary.
- Use your financial literacy in the budgeting of your sports program, and seek insight and assistance from your colleagues and superiors. Avoid adding additional unnecessary financial stressors to the program, and *especially* to the families in your program.

- If fundraising is part of your coaching duties, work to develop competence in using a variety of fundraising options (for example, writing letters seeking financial support, managing auctions or raffles, or operating a fitness challenge event). Build connections and foster relationships with booster clubs and community supporters.

- Act with integrity around all money matters. Carefully manage invoices, receipts, and commitments. Follow all financial policies and stay true to your word when it comes to payment of others.

- Model financial wellness with athletes—not necessarily in relation to your personal finances, but within the bounds of the program. Making fiscally responsible choices is something that can be discussed fairly openly with players of most ages. The concept of living within your means can be modeled through your program.

- Financial wellness should be a consistent consideration on the part of a coach, but be wary of overemphasizing it, because you can end up perpetuating an idea that money and material things are a priority.[4]

TIPS FOR SUPPORTING ATHLETES' FINANCIAL WELLNESS

The following are a few tips to consider to promote financial wellness in athletes:

- Adopt an open-door policy in which athletes and their families feel comfortable discussing financial issues with you. You may not be able to solve anything for them, but the relationship and trust you have built will help alleviate some of the discomfort around discussing finances. You don't want to be in a position in which players are sacrificing their wellness because they are afraid to broach the subject of money with you.

- Finances are a personal matter and should be addressed with compassion and in a way that minimizes the chances anyone will feel ostracized or insecure. Do not make financial issues public—provide options for private discussions.

- Educate yourself about the financial concerns and barriers faced by players. Whether you coach youth, high school, or collegiate athletes, there will be a financial component, and your awareness of their realities will help you to maximize access and minimize associated stressors.

- Remember that financial constraints are not just limited to participation fees. There are costs associated with facilities, uniforms, equipment, travel, meals, team bonding, and the like. A scholarship that simply covers team fees often does not make participation realistic. Take the time to evaluate all of the activities within your program through a lens of financial inclusion. A few actions you may consider taking include: providing a variety of opportunities for families to contribute to the program beyond monetary requests, adjusting practice times so that after-school care for younger siblings is not a barrier, and setting up a system so that uniforms can be washed after each competition. With some awareness and a little creativity, you may find countless options for improving the financial accessibility of your program.
- When establishing plans for camps, tournaments, or other events, consider the financial impact it may have on your program budget.
- Be prepared to discuss sport-related money matters with parents. For many athletes, parents will be carrying the bulk of the burden, and your compassionate approach will go a long way.
- Empathy, empathy, empathy! This is a tough subject. We are operating within a system that has been discriminatory and elitist. Care about your athletes as people, take stock of financial realities, and do your part to contribute to the good of sport culture as a whole.

APPLICATIONS IN COACH DEVELOPMENT: REIMAGINING FINANCIAL STRUCTURES OF SPORT

In the sports world, the financial system we see today has taken decades to develop; however, initiatives to do better are plentiful and gaining momentum.[1] As a coach developer, it is pertinent that you are informed of the trends impacting the sports domain. You may need to help coaches stay informed and, in particular relative to the financial aspect of sports operation, help them to think outside the box. There are a number of innovative programs and practices being used in athletics, and as sports grow more inclusive, such programs will hopefully multiply and eventually become the new norm. Discussions among practitioners with a passion for quality sports programs for all have catapulted such changes into effect, and your continued efforts in this regard are much needed. Keep an open mind to new innovations and continue to foster conversations with leaders in sport, including coaches. Together, we can build a stronger sports system.

Note

1. Ahada McCummings and Caitlin Mance, "USCCE Engagement Event: Community Engagement for Diversified Programming," presented in the United States Center for Coaching Excellence Community Engagement Series, November 19, 2020.

STORIES OF *WINNING WELL* IN FINANCIAL WELLNESS

Malia Kipp

When Malia Kipp was recruited from the Blackfeet Reservation, she was the first female enrolled tribal member to play Division I basketball in Montana. Her success helped open the door to college sports for many aspiring young Indigenous athletes. The financial component of her scholarship was essential; however, it goes beyond just landing her a spot on a college campus. Equipped with expanded opportunities, Malia could afford to explore numerous careers and now serves as a community health nurse for the Salish-Kootenai Tribes.

> Growing up on the reservation, we didn't have much to do in the way of entertainment, but we had the outdoors, our friends and family, and everybody had a basketball. Browning has so many strong athletes and, in the past, Natives were overlooked. Getting the opportunity to go to school on a Division I scholarship was amazing. When I got the call, I played it cool but inside was ecstatic.
>
> There was definitely a lot of pressure on me to prove the typical stereotypes of Native Americans wrong and to serve as a role model. No matter how tired I was or how much I felt like I couldn't do it, quitting was not an option. I had too many youngsters that I needed to motivate. I needed them to know we can be here, we can compete, we can succeed. Natives are resilient people who have overcome many things in the past, and we continue to overcome and educate.

My coach, Rob, was inducted into the Indian Athletic Hall of Fame and is probably one of the only non-Native people to earn that honor. For Native American female athletes, Rob recognized our ability to play at the next level and helped provide us with that opportunity. I remember him really taking the time to get to know me. One of the first times I was in his office, I noticed he had about four books on Native Americans. He was reading about Native Americans because he wanted to have an understanding/appreciation and I assume because he didn't want to offend me in any way. I knew I was valued because Rob took the time to learn.

Getting a four-year scholarship meant so much to me. My parents, at the time, couldn't afford to send me anywhere, so being able to play basketball on a scholarship was what made it possible. Going to school because of basketball brought more to my life than just the game and my classes. I was exposed to different people, a variety of career options, and built a belief in myself that now extended into the classroom as well.

I had never really left Browning before I went to Missoula [for school]; I had only been surrounded by people who I felt understood me, and all of a sudden, there were a lot of different people around. With the opportunities I was presented in college, I was introduced to diversity for the first time. It kind of all weaved into a culture shock and it was really good for me. Everybody needs to see and appreciate diversity—it's important. As a nurse, that is part of my scope of practice. I'm going to meet people with different beliefs. Not judging, listening, and having empathy of where people are allows me to see what I can do to help. I can't push my beliefs on people. If I want to help them, I have to support them and who they are.

I graduated high school when I was seventeen. I had no clue what I was getting into and what I was going to do with myself, but I had always been interested in the human body and health. I wanted to go into sports medicine, and my second semester I had an instructor who told me I wasn't smart enough to be in the medical field. I would love to go back and tell him to look at me now, but honestly, for a second, I believed him too. I changed my major at least three or four times and by the end of my scholarship and my playing years, I hadn't earned my degree from UM.

The time I spent in classes at UM was enough to complete my generals and it showed me what it was I actually wanted to do. Having that scholarship allowed me to explore different fields within medicine that I didn't even know were out there, and I wouldn't have been able to do that without my scholarship. I enrolled at Salish-Kootenai College and became a nurse.

I think being a coach is more than teaching individuals fundamentals, getting them conditioned, or winning games. Being a successful coach means getting to know the people you're working with. Find out their story and share yours. When there is an appreciation of others and their struggles, that's when people unite. They work hard for one another. My coaches knew me and helped provide me with the opportunities I needed to get to where I am today, and I will always be thankful.

Bookie Gates

Bookie Gates came out of the Seattle Central District to play baseball in the major leagues. Grateful for the opportunities he had, which he recognized were not afforded others, he returned to his community and founded Baseball Beyond Borders along with Moving Beyond 12.[5] His programs are geared toward elevating access and opportunities for student-athletes of color. As an essential component of life skills training, Bookie strives to build financial wellness in athletes and families through baseball.

Being an African American growing up in Central Seattle, my life revolved around playing all day on Garfield Playfield. It was a community hub and also ended up being a breeding ground of incredible talent in a variety of sports. There were numerous pro athletes who spent their days on the playfield who were able to navigate the barriers and make it to varying levels of the big leagues. While the place was rife with talent, there were also quite a few athletes who didn't experience that same level of success, not because they didn't have the skills and abilities but specifically because of a lack of access and opportunities. This was particularly true in relation to baseball. It was a little easier to play football or basketball on a school team and get the exposure needed to move on to possibly play college ball, but baseball didn't have those same systems.

Growing up in that situation, coming back to the community, and knowing I was raised by that community gave me great perspective. I grew a passion for trying to find a way to provide opportunities where most of us didn't have them and where most kids don't have them now. I recognized that we had to get out of our community to really experience what baseball could be. When I was pulled away from my community in order to pursue my opportunities in college and the pros, I knew I had an opportunity that was different. I asked myself, how do I bring this back to the community, to kids of color?

Fortunately, for me, my mother worked in the school when I was growing up. She was a registrar, so she understood the process around applying for schools. She had connections with college counselors, she knew the clearinghouse process . . . all of that. Even with that support, there were challenges. If it was difficult for me even though I had a resource, how many others were missing the opportunity? So when we started this, we said, "Let's think holistically." We wanted to get into not just the capacities but the ideologies that are required for student-athletes and families as they navigate postsecondary pathways. Whether they move on as a student-athlete, or a career professional, or both, this is all integral to their success.

We don't want to charge and if we don't have to, we won't. We say to families, pay $200 and if you can pay more, go for it. We don't ask for tax statements or anything like that. The last thing we want is a number to stand in the way of an opportunity for a kid. We want to avoid having a parent pick and choose what they invest in for their child.

The nine innings of Moving Beyond 12 were the essence of what I experienced and what others experienced in preparation for college and careers. It's really a progressive process and each of the competencies builds off of one another. We can't talk about financial literacy if students don't know who they are, how they learn, and what they bring in terms of talents and interests. It's hard to talk about jobs if someone doesn't know their career interests.

Speaking specifically about the financial piece, financial literacy is not just about counting coins. It's about using financial abilities and skills to make informed decisions around money. We can talk all we want about different things you can do to make money, but if you don't have the skills to manage that money, we're missing a very important concept. So that's how we built this progressive framework. We wanted to make sure it was holistic. We wanted them to be able to diversify their portfolio and their capacities.

In our program, we wanted to build that kind of wherewithal for not just students, but families. We need to keep in mind the reality of this for our student-athletes because they are still at home. Sometimes their home reality doesn't match what we are teaching, which makes it that much more important that we include parents—the forever coach. Installing understandings and instilling confidence for everyone around money is important.

We think of it as planting seeds in the parents to have the understanding and capacity to begin to implement financial literacy, because that's where the teaching for student-athletes begins. We can't fault the parents on all of this because they were never taught—the current educational system doesn't emphasize financial literacy. Parents don't know what they don't know. We want parents to feel equipped with the tools and the financial efficacy they need. While we are teaching them, they are doing it together. They build a community to work with. They can learn with each other and community efficacy builds in the process. People overlook these elements of the importance of community. Even these competencies are all a part of the natural conversations that we create. It's no different than what is being spoken about in a barber shop. It comes out in different forms and ways. It's the conversations that should be happening around the dinner table.

We start by talking about what it means to have a bank account and then elevate it to money management. We give them the spectrum and open their mind to possibility—the gamut of what financial literacy really brings. We facilitate workshops and others come in to teach. We go through what financial aid means and what they need to know. We'll teach them that it all has to do with grants and loans and what those things mean. If I'm a student-athlete and I want to pursue postsecondary education, how do I go about that process if I don't know what my options are? We host CPAs, others in money management, and even sometimes business owners come in to speak from a real-time perspective. They'll tell us what they've done, how they run their business, and what they had to learn. They may not have gone to college, but they own a business and they'll talk about how they learned how to manage financials.

We had one student who was very intrigued by Jed Collins (a former NFL player), who came in to speak, and he was teaching student-athletes about money management. He told the students that he got his first big paycheck and didn't know what to do with it. He walked players through the whole process of what he learned and what he did as a result. He told the kids to ask their parents to purchase them something in the [stock] market as opposed to an Xbox, explaining what happens over the years. Jed's insight opened one of our student-athletes' eyes. Later his mom sent a message saying, "Thank you. I don't know what you did with my son, but he's now asking for this and that [investment], and it's not an Xbox anymore." We aren't saying everyone is going to go invest in the market, but when you plant those seeds in them, they are informed and can make that decision down the road when they do make the money to invest.

Here baseball is the avenue for us in showing that we care about the individual. We care more about someone coming back to tell us that they have become a CEO than we would if they came back to tell us they were a top draft pick. We get great joy out of the times we are asked to be a reference on a job application or for approval on a mortgage. The athletes know we care about them as a person and want to see them succeed beyond sports. For us, this goes beyond the foul lines and into the homes, classrooms, etc. Baseball is the vehicle that helps them to grow to be a better person and navigate the world, including the financial aspects.

Being able to give back to my community like this is the greatest feeling. As a young athlete, I heard about the stars, and always had in the back of my mind that if I got there, I would make the community better than when I left it. Now I'm doing it and it can't get any better than that.

10

Conclusion

Working with people, we will constantly encounter moments of strife and moments of glory. There is a rollercoaster involved in the life of a coach that cannot be denied, especially for coaches who push themselves to do the most good possible. Your commitment to work through these challenges helps to improve the lives of athletes, and ultimately, the culture of sports. Some days and with some athletes it will feel like a breeze, and with others and under different circumstances, it may present a formidable task. Ultimately, it is your efforts that matter most, that will always make a difference, and for which you are most appreciated.

The opportunity to coach athletes is a gift. They come to us nervous and/or excited, unsure and/or beaming with confidence, and with varying levels of trust in our commitment to their experience being a positive one. While the variety in what each person brings to sports is immeasurable, there is one universal truth: Each of us, athletes and coaches alike, comes to sports as a person—a whole person who lives their life along with their sport. We bring our identities, past experiences, and hopes to the game.

Using wellness as a framework allows us to bring all aspects of a person to light. It provides the flexibility to bring a different focal point to each person's experience, and it is constantly evolving with the world around us. Sports can provide stability amid chaos, while acknowledging the complexities of life builds a platform for success for everyone involved. We don't get to separate our sports skills into a box and leave all the rest behind. Athletics are not played in a lab, and as a result, things are always changing, there is always much to learn, and the potential for new victories is always around the corner.

All athletes and coaches have a right to life-changing involvement in the game. This is possible in all contexts and conditions by maintaining focus on what *really* matters—the people. Authentically engaging in wellness is a life-long process with the possibility of fantastic results. When employing tactics to maximize wellness in yourself and the athletes you coach, your work is never done. It is easy to view all of this and feel overwhelmed or insufficient due to the endless potential for growth, but it is that aspect of the model that is most energizing. There is considerable flexibility in this work along with the ability to personalize priorities, adjust your approaches, and address what is most meaningful to athletes with genuine timing and tact. Using wellness as your guide, you can efficiently and effectively work with others to bring out their very best, at any given time, both on and off the field of play. Your long-term commitment to this process creates champions for life.

Sport-specific teaching skills and expertise will always play an important role in coaching. Efforts put into growing that capacity will certainly support your craft. Investing in wellness for everyone—building on inclusion and valuing each individual's right to be coached as a whole person—virtually guarantees success. As part of striving for excellence, competing to win heightens your capacity for impact, and wins and losses play an important role in driving the holistic growth process. How that looks will be different for each and every one of us, and what we take away will vary just as much, but these are the hallmarks of winning programs.

Your legacy as a coach can be expressed in athletes' responses to the questions: What did your coach teach you? How have their efforts impacted your life? There is well-deserved pride to feel from wellness-enhancing efforts employed in coaching. Through a focus on the humans who put their trust in your hands, you can see great success in ways that are far reaching and life-altering. When you commit to winning well, you and the athletes you coach are able to realize a healthy and happy level of wellness while thriving in their sport.

Game on!

Appendix A
Wellness Wheel Activity

This assessment can be completed to evaluate your current personal wellness or support for athlete wellness. If you are evaluating your personal wellness, complete the entire wheel based on your personal wellness. If you are evaluating your support for athlete wellness, complete the entire wheel based on your support for athlete wellness.

For each of the dimensions of wellness, mark a point on each corresponding line to indicate a score of 0 to 10 (10 being the best it could possibly be). After you have marked your score for each dimension, connect the points to form your wellness wheel.

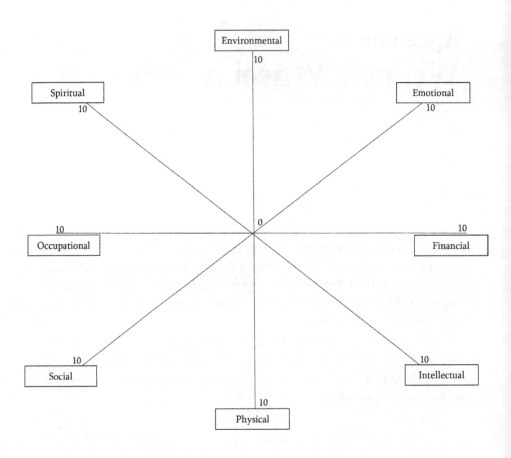

Appendix B
Wellness Wheel Assessments by Dimension

The following assessments address aspects pertinent to maximizing each dimension of your personal wellness and your support for athlete wellness. The prompts are intended to increase your awareness and may bring to light areas for improvement. The goal is for you to reflect on current choices and behaviors that impact your wellness and the wellness of the athletes you coach.

To use these assessments in conjunction with the wellness wheel, complete the following steps:

- Select the most accurate response for each of the prompts in the chart below and award yourself with the corresponding number of points.
- Total your points for all prompts combined.
- Divide the total number of points by 3 to find your comprehensive score for each dimension of wellness.
- Plot your score for each dimension of wellness on the wellness wheel.

Physical Wellness Assessment Tool, Coach's Personal Wellness

Physical Wellness Prompts	Never or Rarely	Sometimes	Regularly or Always
I move my body throughout the day.	1	2	3
I make conscious decisions to consume foods that maximize my health and fuel my body efficiently.	1	2	3
I take my time with meals and enjoy the food I'm eating.	1	2	3
I do not judge my body based on societal expectations or comparisons to others, and I appreciate what my body does for me.	1	2	3
I minimize my consumption of alcohol and other drugs not prescribed by a doctor.	1	2	3
I do not rely on caffeine or other stimulants to make it through my days.	1	2	3
I maintain a reasonable sleep schedule, getting at least eight hours of sleep each night.	1	2	3
I minimize late-night distractions and electronics to enhance the quality of my sleep.	1	2	3
I am aware of the physical signs of stress on my body.	1	2	3
I evaluate how my beliefs, behaviors, and choices impact my physical wellness.	1	2	3
Total number of points for all prompts combined:			
Comprehensive score for physical wellness (divide total points by 3):			

Physical Wellness Assessment Tool, Coach Support for Athlete Wellness

Physical Wellness Prompts	Never or Rarely	Sometimes	Regularly or Always
I model staying active, fueling my body for performance, and prioritizing sleep.	1	2	3
I purposefully plan training sessions based on principles of training and athletes' responses to training.	1	2	3
I prioritize safety, and I encourage athletes to listen to their bodies and be transparent about their injuries.	1	2	3
I balance deliberate practice and deliberate play to maximize learning and enjoyment.	1	2	3
I constantly monitor my messaging around food and body shape and size, while promoting body positivity for athletes.	1	2	3
I refer to experts and current best practices in relation to physical training and nutrition.	1	2	3
I directly address substance use and abuse with athletes and ensure that related policies are clear. *If this does not apply to your age group, award yourself 3 points for this prompt.*	1	2	3
I directly address the need for sleep and promote healthy sleeping habits for athletes.	1	2	3
I promote healthy, effective stress management behaviors in athletes.	1	2	3
I follow protocol in my role as a mandatory reporter.	1	2	3
Total number of points for all prompts combined:			
Comprehensive score for physical wellness (divide total points by 3):			

Social Wellness Assessment Tool, Coach's Personal Wellness

Social Wellness Prompts	Never or Rarely	Sometimes	Regularly or Always
I demonstrate empathy and promote inclusion in all of my social interactions.	1	2	3
I am fully engaged and present with my loved ones when I spend time with them.	1	2	3
I ensure that my friends and family know they are a priority to me, regardless of my coaching duties.	1	2	3
I maintain a support system specifically to help me manage the challenges associated with coaching.	1	2	3
I build authentic, respectful relationships with my coaching staff and others involved in the administration of my program.	1	2	3
My interactions with opposing coaches, game officials, and league administrators are professional and positive.	1	2	3
I build trusting, respectful relationships with athletes.	1	2	3
I maintain clear, appropriate boundaries in relationships with athletes.	1	2	3
I prioritize enjoyment and personal growth in social interactions with athletes, coaches, and others involved in the administration of my program.	1	2	3
I build effective, positive connections with athletes' families.	1	2	3
Total number of points for all prompts combined:			
Comprehensive score for social wellness (divide total points by 3):			

Social Wellness Assessment Tool, Coach Support for Athlete Wellness

Social Wellness Prompts	Never or Rarely	Sometimes	Regularly or Always
I model empathy, inclusion, and positive social interactions.	1	2	3
I prioritize getting to know athletes as people.	1	2	3
I create and reinforce a safe, supportive, and welcoming environment for all.	1	2	3
I guide athletes to maintain a safe, supportive, and welcoming environment for all.	1	2	3
I guide athletes to consistently communicate with one another in a positive, respectful manner.	1	2	3
I guide athletes to maintain safe, healthy relationships in all aspects of their lives.	1	2	3
I employ age-appropriate team-building tactics to help maximize team cohesion.	1	2	3
I directly address the pros and cons of social media and help athletes to use it in a positive manner.	1	2	3
I engage parents appropriately to help maximize athlete and program success.	1	2	3
I clearly communicate program expectations to all involved.	1	2	3
Total number of points for all prompts combined:			
Comprehensive score for social wellness (divide total points by 3):			

Emotional Wellness Assessment Tool, Coach's Personal Wellness

Emotional Wellness Prompts	Never or Rarely	Sometimes	Regularly or Always
I allow myself to fully experience all of the different emotions I feel.	1	2	3
I do not judge the emotions I feel as bad/good or wrong/right.	1	2	3
I express my emotions in a manner that does not cause harm to myself or others.	1	2	3
I practice mindfulness and/or intentionally focus on living in the moment.	1	2	3
I do not associate expressing emotion with weakness in myself.	1	2	3
I appropriately manage stress so that it does not have a negative impact on my coaching.	1	2	3
I appropriately manage stress associated with coaching so that it does not have a negative impact on my personal life and my loved ones.	1	2	3
I recognize the value of and need for emotions in sports.	1	2	3
I advocate for mental health in sports.	1	2	3
I am open to referring to mental health professionals as needed and/or desired to maximize my personal wellness.	1	2	3
Total number of points for all prompts combined:			
Comprehensive score for emotional wellness (divide total points by 3):			

Emotional Wellness Assessment Tool, Coach Support for Athlete Wellness

Emotional Wellness Prompts	Never or Rarely	Sometimes	Regularly or Always
I model acknowledging, experiencing, and expressing both comfortable and uncomfortable emotions.	1	2	3
I directly address the courage, value, and importance of athletes expressing emotion in sports, performance, and life.	1	2	3
I guide athletes to express emotions in a manner that does not cause harm to themselves or others.	1	2	3
I demonstrate empathy with athletes' emotions.	1	2	3
I maintain an environment that is safe and supportive for athletes to express emotions.	1	2	3
I interact with athletes in a manner to purposefully build their self-esteem.	1	2	3
I prioritize the fun in sports and create opportunities for enjoyment for athletes.	1	2	3
I directly address the benefits of practicing mindfulness and/or guide athletes in mindful activities.	1	2	3
I am aware of the resources available to me and am prepared to follow policies and procedures in relation to mental health emergencies for athletes.	1	2	3
I am cognizant of any behaviors in athletes that may indicate a risk for suicide.	1	2	3
Total number of points for all prompts combined:			
Comprehensive score for emotional wellness (divide total points by 3):			

Intellectual Wellness Assessment Tool, Coach's Personal Wellness

Intellectual Wellness Prompts	Never or Rarely	Sometimes	Regularly or Always
I embrace my own curiosity and seek out opportunities to learn.	1	2	3
Continuing to learn throughout my life is important to me.	1	2	3
I give my best effort and expect to make mistakes in the process.	1	2	3
I am eager to learn from my mistakes.	1	2	3
I participate in coach development opportunities, both formal and informal.	1	2	3
I reflect on my coaching practices to improve.	1	2	3
I am aware of my coaching strengths and strive to maximize them.	1	2	3
I am aware of my coaching weaknesses and work to improve in those areas.	1	2	3
I use visualization to help me improve my coaching.	1	2	3
When I am coaching, I am fully engaged in the present moment.	1	2	3
Total number of points for all prompts combined:			
Comprehensive score for intellectual wellness (divide total points by 3):			

Intellectual Wellness Assessment Tool, Coach Support for Athlete Wellness

Intellectual Wellness Prompts	Never or Rarely	Sometimes	Regularly or Always
I model a growth mindset for athletes, striving for excellence as opposed to perfection.	1	2	3
I create opportunities for athletes to be challenged at the peak of their abilities and foster an appreciation for mistakes as opportunities for growth.	1	2	3
I prioritize the long-term value of athletes' efforts over their successes and failures.	1	2	3
I guide athletes to focus on the current moment while practicing and competing.	1	2	3
I use feedback to purposefully build skills, understanding, and confidence in athletes.	1	2	3
I provide opportunities and guidance for athletes to make use of reflection to improve performance.	1	2	3
I encourage athletes to identify their motivation(s) for participating in sport.	1	2	3
I guide athletes to develop a thorough understanding of the skills, strategies, and tactics of the sport.	1	2	3
I encourage and guide athletes to use visualization to improve performance.	1	2	3
I promote athletes' individual academic and career/life goals and recognize their growth.	1	2	3
Total number of points for all prompts combined:			
Comprehensive score for intellectual wellness (divide total points by 3):			

Spiritual Wellness Assessment Tool, Coach's Personal Wellness

Spiritual Wellness Prompts	Never or Rarely	Sometimes	Regularly or Always
My personal core values are very clear to me.	1	2	3
I demonstrate my core values through my choices and behaviors.	1	2	3
The core values I espouse in coaching are very clear to me.	1	2	3
The core values I espouse in coaching are very clear to my coaching staff and the athletes I coach.	1	2	3
When facing an ethical dilemma in sports, my core values serve as my guide.	1	2	3
I ensure that my coaching philosophy fits who I am as a person.	1	2	3
I reevaluate my coaching philosophy each season, and as I learn and develop, I adjust my coaching philosophy accordingly.	1	2	3
I proudly share my coaching philosophy with athletes' families and others invested in my program.	1	2	3
I feel inspired and motivated to coach.	1	2	3
I am grounded in purpose beyond myself, the athletes I coach, and my sport.	1	2	3
Total number of points for all prompts combined:			
Comprehensive score for spiritual wellness (divide total points by 3):			

Spiritual Wellness Assessment Tool, Coach Support for Athlete Wellness

Spiritual Wellness Prompts	Never or Rarely	Sometimes	Regularly or Always
I demonstrate inclusion and support for all forms of spirituality.	1	2	3
I guide athletes to demonstrate inclusion and support for all forms of spirituality.	1	2	3
I provide opportunities to celebrate all forms of spirituality within my program.	1	2	3
My core values are clear to people both inside and outside of my program.	1	2	3
I directly address the application of core values with athletes, both in and out of sport.	1	2	3
I select specific character traits and explicitly guide athletes in their development throughout the season (e.g., using lessons geared toward specifically teaching integrity).	1	2	3
I guide athletes to practice ethical decision making.	1	2	3
I ensure that team goals, discussions, awards, etc. are aligned with the core values of the program.	1	2	3
I use each athlete's unique motivational preferences to coach them most effectively.	1	2	3
I strive to empower athletes for long-term success by cultivating intrinsic motivation.	1	2	3
Total number of points for all prompts combined:			
Comprehensive score for spiritual wellness (divide total points by 3):			

Environmental Wellness Assessment Tool, Coach's Personal Wellness

Environmental Wellness Prompts	Never or Rarely	Sometimes	Regularly or Always
I recognize and value factors in the environment that influence my overall wellness.	1	2	3
I am aware of the factors that I *can* control or influence in the environment.	1	2	3
I maintain healthy, clean, organized spaces to maximize my efficiency.	1	2	3
I intentionally invest effort toward demonstrating professionalism in my coaching environment.	1	2	3
I engage with the broader community in which I coach.	1	2	3
My actions demonstrate the culture I have established in my program.	1	2	3
I seek feedback about how my program identity is interpreted by others.	1	2	3
I strive to purposefully bring positive energy to all environments.	1	2	3
I create environments that allow me to enjoy coaching.	1	2	3
I demonstrate professionalism and promote my program identity through my actions outside of my coaching environment.	1	2	3
Total number of points for all prompts combined:			
Comprehensive score for environmental wellness (divide total points by 3):			

Environmental Wellness Assessment Tool, Coach Support for Athlete Wellness

Environmental Wellness Prompts	Never or Rarely	Sometimes	Regularly or Always
I build an environment that holistically supports my program culture.	1	2	3
I employ routines with athletes that reinforce the program culture.	1	2	3
I ensure that verbal and nonverbal messages in my coaching environment are consistent with the core values of the program.	1	2	3
My feedback for athletes is specific and positively worded to maximize clarity and support.	1	2	3
I guide athletes to take care of and build pride in all of the environments we enter.	1	2	3
I am aware of the energy of the group and strive to maximize its positive influence.	1	2	3
I prioritize the wellness and safety of athletes in all environments.	1	2	3
I identify and create opportunities for athletes to contribute to the broader community.	1	2	3
I make a conscious effort to promote my sport in general, with athletes.	1	2	3
I engage parents in positively contributing to the program identity.	1	2	3
Total number of points for all prompts combined:			
Comprehensive score for environmental wellness (divide total points by 3):			

Occupational Wellness Assessment Tool, Coach's Personal Wellness

Occupational Wellness Prompts	Never or Rarely	Sometimes	Regularly or Always
I feel inspired and/or fulfilled in my coaching role.	1	2	3
I maintain boundaries, in relation to the time I spend coaching, that enhance my overall wellness.	1	2	3
I ensure that my identity as a person is not entirely based on my coaching role.	1	2	3
I ensure that my energy in coaching is dedicated to aspects that I can control.	1	2	3
I purposefully implement a variety of coaching strategies and/or engage with new strategies to maintain inspiration.	1	2	3
I strive to keep sports and coaching in perspective.	1	2	3
The people in my coaching support system promote my overall wellness.	1	2	3
My values and priorities are shared by the people in my coaching support system.	1	2	3
I seek opportunities to celebrate even small successes in coaching.	1	2	3
I promote the coaching profession for others.	1	2	3
Total number of points for all prompts combined:			
Comprehensive score for occupational wellness (divide total points by 3):			

Occupational Wellness Assessment Tool, Coach Support for Athlete Wellness

Occupational Wellness Prompts	Never or Rarely	Sometimes	Regularly or Always
I communicate my personal/professional life boundaries with athletes and families.	1	2	3
I demonstrate my personal/professional life boundaries with athletes and families.	1	2	3
I outwardly express joy and satisfaction in my role as a coach.	1	2	3
I explicitly guide athletes in the development of work-related skills.	1	2	3
I appropriately share my perspective and experiences in coaching with athletes to promote the profession.	1	2	3
I promote opportunities for athletes to coach.	1	2	3
I promote occupational opportunities for athletes through all aspects of sport (e.g., officiating and game management).	1	2	3
I support and seek opportunities to celebrate the academic and career aspirations of all athletes.	1	2	3
I promote athletes' appreciation for their identity as a person—both in and out of sport.	1	2	3
I demonstrate empathy and prioritize support for athletes and coaches ending their careers.	1	2	3
Total number of points for all prompts combined:			
Comprehensive score for occupational wellness (divide total points by 3):			

Financial Wellness Assessment Tool, Coach's Personal Wellness

Financial Wellness Prompts	Never or Rarely	Sometimes	Regularly or Always
I am honest with myself about my own financial situation and avoid comparing my finances to others'.	1	2	3
I spend less than I earn each month.	1	2	3
I strive to expand my financial literacy.	1	2	3
I am able to avoid stress about the amount I am paid for coaching.	1	2	3
I carefully budget for my program according to current resources.	1	2	3
I have developed adequate fundraising skills and initiatives to support my fundraising duties. *If this does not apply to your coaching role, award yourself 3 points for this prompt.*	1	2	3
I act with and prioritize integrity in relation to all financial components of my coaching role while following all expected protocols. *If this does not apply to your coaching role, award yourself 3 points for this prompt.*	1	2	3
I build positive connections with boosters, the community, and other sources of financial support and resources for my program. *If this does not apply to your coaching role, award yourself 3 points for this prompt.*	1	2	3
According to the context in which I coach, I emphasize financial components appropriately without perpetuating the idea that money and material things are priorities.	1	2	3
I am aware of systemic financial barriers in sport and promote improvements in the system.	1	2	3
Total number of points for all prompts combined:			
Comprehensive score for financial wellness (divide total points by 3):			

Financial Wellness Assessment Tool, Coach Support for Athlete Wellness

Financial Wellness Prompts	Never or Rarely	Sometimes	Regularly or Always
I ensure that athletes feel comfortable discussing their financial concerns with me.	1	2	3
I am aware of the financial realities of all athletes in my program.	1	2	3
I consider the potential financial impacts on athletes, families, and the program budget when making decisions.	1	2	3
I strive to minimize financial hardship associated with participation fees in my program.	1	2	3
I strive to minimize financial hardship and logistical barriers associated with athletes' equipment/gear needs and maintenance.	1	2	3
I am aware of athletes' feasibility to fuel their bodies for performance and seek support for them as needed.	1	2	3
I minimize the barriers families may encounter associated with practice times, locations, and all other logistics in my program.	1	2	3
I compassionately discuss sport-related money matters with families.	1	2	3
I approach financial issues with empathy.	1	2	3
I work toward minimizing systemic financial barriers in sport for all athletes.	1	2	3
Total number of points for all prompts combined:			
Comprehensive score for financial wellness (divide total points by 3):			

Appendix C
BIPOC (Black, Indigenous, and People of Color) Inclusion Assessment Tool

The following assessment addresses aspects pertinent to inclusion related to BIPOC. The prompts are intended to increase your awareness and may bring to light areas for improvement. The goal is for you to reflect on current choices and behaviors that impact the inclusive or exclusive nature of your work as a coach.

BIPOC Inclusion Prompts	Never or Rarely	Sometimes	Regularly or Always
In all settings, I am aware of my race and intersectional identity and what it may communicate to others.	1	2	3
I actively strive to identify my personal biases around race.	1	2	3
I engage in difficult or uncomfortable conversations about racism with others.	1	2	3
When I encounter something I don't understand about race-related topics and issues, I take the initiative to educate myself (without tokenizing others).	1	2	3
I listen to BIPOC perspectives; support BIPOC leaders, businesses, and organizations; and consume products and media created by BIPOC.	1	2	3
I recognize systemic barriers for BIPOC in sports, including in my own program.	1	2	3
I ensure a safe environment for individuals of all racial identities in my program.	1	2	3
I promote racially inclusive behaviors among my coaching staff, athletes, families, and others involved in the administration of my program.	1	2	3
I use BIPOC perspectives to employ inclusion as a guiding principle in my coaching.	1	2	3
The actions I take as a coach demonstrate a strong, authentic commitment to BIPOC inclusion.	1	2	3
I vocally (at minimum) support programs, organizations, and individuals that advance BIPOC inclusion in sports.	1	2	3
I actively work to increase BIPOC inclusion in coaching and leadership roles in sports.	1	2	3
I am committed to continuing to learn and grow as a person and coach in relation to BIPOC inclusion and will implement increasing inclusion in my program.	1	2	3
Total number of points for all prompts combined:			
Rating for BIPOC inclusion (divide total points by 3.9, for a possible high score of 10):			

Appendix D

Gender and LGBTQ2+ (Lesbian, Gay, Bisexual, Transgender, Queer/ Questioning, Two-Spirit, and other Sexual Orientations and Gender Identities) Inclusion Assessment Tool

The following assessment addresses aspects pertinent to inclusion related to gender and the LGBTQ2+ community. The prompts are intended to increase your awareness and may bring to light areas for improvement. The goal is for you to reflect on current choices and behaviors that impact the inclusive or exclusive nature of your work as a coach.

Gender and LGBTQ2+ Inclusion Prompts	Never or Rarely	Sometimes	Regularly or Always
In all settings, I am aware of my gender and intersectional identity and what it may communicate to others.	1	2	3
I actively strive to identify my personal biases around gender and sexual identities.	1	2	3
I engage in difficult or uncomfortable conversations about sexism, transphobia, and homophobia with others.	1	2	3
When I encounter something I don't understand about LGBTQ2+ topics and issues, I take the initiative to educate myself (without tokenizing others).	1	2	3
I recognize systemic barriers based on gender and LGBTQ2+ identity in sports, including in my own program.	1	2	3
I ensure a safe environment for individuals of all sexual orientations and gender identities in my program.	1	2	3
I promote LGBTQ2+-inclusive behaviors among my coaching staff, athletes, families, and others involved in the administration of my program.	1	2	3
I use gender diverse and LGBTQ2+ perspectives to employ inclusion as a guiding principle in my coaching.	1	2	3
The actions I take as a coach demonstrate a strong, authentic commitment to gender and LGBTQ2+ inclusion.	1	2	3
I vocally (at minimum) support programs, organizations, and individuals that advance gender and LGBTQ2+ inclusion in sports.	1	2	3
I actively work to increase gender diversity and LGBTQ2+ inclusion in coaching and leadership roles in sports.	1	2	3
I am committed to continuing to learn and grow as a person and coach in relation to gender and LGBTQ2+ inclusion and will implement increasing inclusion in my program.	1	2	3
Total number of points for all prompts combined:			
Rating for gender and LGBTQ2+ inclusion (divide total points by 3.6, for a possible high score of 10):			

Notes

INTRODUCTION

1. Amanda J. Visek, Sara M. Achrati, Heather M. Mannix, Karen McDonnell, Brandonn S. Harris, and Loretta DiPietro, "The Fun Integration Theory: Toward Sustaining Children and Adolescents Sport Participation," *Journal of Physical Activity & Health* 12, no. 3 (2015): 424–33, https://doi.org/10.1123/jpah.2013-0180.

2. Jeffrey J. Huber, *Applying Educational Psychology in Coaching Athletes* (Champaign, IL: Human Kinetics, 2013).

3. Charles H. Wilson and Trey Burdette, "Holistic, Athlete-Centered Coaching Orientation," in *Coach Education Essentials: Your Guide to Developing Sport Coaches*, edited by Kristen Dieffenbach and Melissa Thompson (Champaign, IL: Human Kinetics, 2020), 35–50.

4. Simon Sinek, *The Infinite Game* (Self-published, Portfolio, 2019).

5. Bo Hanson, "Application in Practice," 169–70, quoted in Cameron Kiosoglous, "Coach Education of Professional- and Olympic-Level Coaches," in *Coach Education Essentials: Your Guide to Developing Sport Coaches*, edited by Kristen Dieffenbach and Melissa Thompson (Champaign, IL: Human Kinetics, 2020), 155–70.

6. Tomaz Lasic, "Maslow before Bloom," *Edublogs* (blog), November 8, 2009, https://human.edublogs.org/2009/08/11/maslow-before-bloom/.

7. United States Olympic and Paralympic Committee, *Quality Coaching Framework* (2020), https://www.teamusa.org/About-the-USOPC/Programs/Coaching-Education/Quality-Coaching-Framework.

8. Hanson, "Application in Practice," 169.

9. James M. Kouzes and Barry Z. Posner, "Leadership Begins with an Inner Journey," *Leader to Leader* 60 (2011): 22–27, https://doi.org/10.1002/ltl.464.

10. Parker J. Palmer, *The Courage to Teach: Exploring the Inner Landscape of a Teacher's Life* (San Francisco, CA: Jossey-Bass, 2007).

11. University of Washington, Center for Leadership in Athletics, *Center for Leadership in Athletics, University of Washington: Where Education, Sport, and Research Converge* (2018), http://uwcla.uw.edu/.

12. Brenè Brown, *Dare to Lead* (New York: Penguin Random House, 2018).

13. National Wellness Institute, *The Six Dimensions of Wellness* (2019), https://nationalwellness.org/resources/six-dimensions-of-wellness/.

14. Dan Beuttner, *Thrive: Finding Happiness the Blue Zones Way* (Washington, DC: National Geographic, 2010).

15. Substance Abuse and Mental Health Services Administration, *Creating a Healthier Life: A Step-by-Step Guide to Wellness* (2016), https://store.samhsa.gov/sites/default/files/d7/priv/sma16-4958.pdf.

CHAPTER 1

1. Aspen Institute, Project Play, https://www.aspenprojectplay.org/.

2. Gabriela Morgado de Oliveira Coelho, Ainà Innocencio da Silva Gomes, Beatriz Gonçalves Ribeiro, and Eliane de Abreu Soares, "Prevention of Eating Disorders in Female Athletes," *Journal of Sports Medicine* 5 (2014): 105–13, https://doi.org/10.2147/OAJSM.S36528.

3. Julie Church, Marsa Daniel, and Julie McCleery, "Creating a Healthy Sports Culture: Facilitating Athletes' Positive Relationship with Food and Body," presented at Collaborative Workshop by Opal: Food & Body Wisdom, University of Washington Center for Leadership in Athletics, and Marsa Daniel, Seattle, Washington, January 11, 2020.

4. Mary Cain and Michel Martin, "Pro Runner Mary Cain Discusses Abuse Allegations against Nike," *All Things Considered*, produced by NPR, November 17, 2019 (podcast), http://https://www.npr.org/2019/11/17/780312550/pro-runner-mary-cain-discusses-abuse-allegations-against-nike.

5. Ellyn Satter Institute, https://www.ellynsatterinstitute.org/.

6. Matthew Walker, *Why We Sleep: Unlocking the Power of Sleep and Dreams* (New York: Scribner, 2017).

7. Lauren Fleshman, "Opinion: I Changed My Body for My Sport. No Girl Should," *New York Times*, November 16, 2019, https://www.nytimes .com/2019/11/16/opinion/girls-sports.html?smid=fb-nytopinion&smtyp=cur&fbclid =IwAR2Tat3Je8Q1qmA4uoU3pGcYz-Cm7gRNbzjjuz5Ga7gZEhMKnEoBpPegx64.

8. SHAPE America, "National Standards for Sport Coaches," https://www .shapeamerica.org/standards/coaching/.

9. Jean Côté, Joseph Baker, and Bruce Abernethy, "From Play to Practice: A Developmental Framework for the Acquisition of Expertise in Team Sport," in *Expert Performance in Sports: Advances in Research on Sport Expertise*, edited by Janet L. Starkes and K. Anders Ericsson (Champaign, IL: Human Kinetics, 2003), 89–113.

10. John Kessel, "'Ancora Imparo'—Secrets Learned in 50 Years of Coaching around the World," keynote address at the United States Center for Coaching Excellence 2019 Summit, Colorado Springs, Colorado, June 18, 2019.

11. Istvan Balyi, Richard Way, and Colin Higgs, *Long-Term Athlete Development* (Champaign, IL: Human Kinetics, 2013).

12. Marty Gaal, "7 Principles of Exercise and Sport Training," Team USA (2012), https://www.teamusa.org/USA-Triathlon/News/Blogs/Multisport-Lab/2012/ August/28/7-Principles-of-Exercise-and-Sport-Training#:~:text=The%20 principles%20of%20specificity%2C%20progression,want%20to%20improve%20you-r%20performance; *Oxford English Dictionary: The Definitive Record of the English Language* (2020), https://www.oed.com/.

13. NCAA Sport Science Institute, *Nutrition, Sleep, and Performance Educational Resources* (2019), http://www.ncaa.org/sport-science-institute/nutrition-sleep-and-performance-educational-resources.

14. Stacey T. Sims and Selene Yeager, *ROAR: How to Match Your Food and Fitness to Your Unique Female Physiology for Optimum Performance, Great Health, and a Strong, Lean Body for Life* (New York: Rodale, 2016).

15. Kathryn E. Ackerman, Trent Stellingwerff, Kirsty J. Elliott-Sale, Amy Baltzell, Mary Cain, Kara Goucher, Lauren Fleshman, and Margo L. Mountjoy, "#REDS (Relative Energy Deficiency in Sport): Time for a Revolution in Sports Culture and Systems to Improve Athlete Health and Performance," *British Journal of Sports Medicine* 54, no. 7 (2020): 369–70, https://doi.org/10.1136/bjsports-2019-101926.

16. Church, Daniel, and McCleery, "Creating a Healthy Sports Culture: Facilitating Athletes' Positive Relationship with Food and Body."

17. National Eating Disorders Association, https://www.nationaleatingdisorders.org/.

18. Caitlyn Fuller, Eric Lehman, Steven Hicks, and Marsha B. Novick, "Bedtime Use of Technology and Associated Sleep Problems in Children." *Global Pediatric Health* (2017), https://www.ncbi.nlm.nih.gov/pmc/articles/PMC5669315/.

19. National Domestic Violence Hotline, https://www.thehotline.org/.

20. U.S. Department of Health and Human Services, "Child Abuse and Neglect," Children's Bureau: An Office of the Administration for Children and Families (2019), https://www.acf.hhs.gov/cb/focus-areas/child-abuse-neglect.

21. National Coalition Against Domestic Violence, https://ncadv.org/.

22. U.S. Center for SafeSport. https://uscenterforsafesport.org/.

CHAPTER 2

1. University of California, Davis, Student Health and Counseling Services, *What Is Wellness?* (2019), https://shcs.ucdavis.edu/wellness/what-is-wellness.

2. Jessica Martino, Jennifer Pegg, and Elizabeth Pegg Frates, "The Connection Prescription: Using the Power of Social Interactions and the Deep Desire for Connectedness to Empower Health and Wellness," *American Journal of Lifestyle Medicine* 11, no. 6 (2015): 466–75, https://doi.org/10.1177/1559827615608788.

3. Sophia Jowett, "Coaching Effectiveness: The Coach-Athlete Relationship at Its Heart," *Current Opinion in Psychology* 16 (2017): 154–58, https://doi.org/10.1016/j.copsyc.2017.05.006.

4. James MacGregor Burns, *Leadership* (New York: Harper & Row, 1978).

5. Peter M. Senge, *The Fifth Discipline: The Art and Practice of the Learning Organization*, 2nd ed. (New York: Doubleday, 2006).

6. Wade Gilbert, *Coaching Better Every Season: A Year-Round System for Athlete Development and Program Success* (Champaign, IL: Human Kinetics, 2017).

7. Valorie Kondos Field, "Why Winning Doesn't Always Equal Success," TEDWomen, December 20, 2019, https://www.ted.com/talks/valorie_kondos_field_why_winning_doesn_t_always_equal_success/transcript?language=en.

8. Chenghao Ma, "The Impact of Social Media," *Sport Digest*, November 21, 2018, http://thesportdigest.com/2018/11/the-impact-of-social-media-in-sports/.

9. Daniel Gould and Jenny Nalepa, "Coaching Club and Scholastic Sports," in *Coach Education Essentials: Your Guide to Developing Sport Coaches*, edited by Kristen Dieffenbach and Melissa Thompson (Champaign, IL: Human Kinetics, 2020), 125.

10. Julie McCleery, "Dr. Julie McCleery: Building Bridges with Parents," produced by Center for Leadership in Athletics, University of Washington, *Ambitious Coaching Podcast,* fall 2018, https://soundcloud.com/user-617023187/building_bridges_launch_version.

CHAPTER 3

1. Matthew Stevens, "Sports Are a Microcosm of Today's Broken Society," *Fan Nation,* June 1, 2020, https://www.si.com/college/illinois/olympic-sports/illini-now-matthew-stevens-column-society-and-sports-june-1-2020.

2. Jennifer S. Lerner, Ye Li, Piercarlo Valdesolo, and Karim S. Kassam, "Emotion and Decision Making," *Annual Review of Psychology* 66, no. 1 (2015): 799–823, https://doi.org/10.1146/annurev-psych-010213-115043.

3. Lori Gottlieb, *Maybe You Should Talk to Someone: A Therapist, HER Therapist, and Our Lives Revealed* (Boston: Houghton Mifflin Harcourt, 2019), 8.

4. James M. Kouzes and Barry Z. Posner, "Leadership Begins with an Inner Journey," *Leader to Leader* 60 (2011): 22–27, https://doi.org/10.1002/ltl.464.

5. Jennifer Siebel Newsom, dir. *The Mask You Live In* [DVD] (San Francisco: Representation Project, 2015).

6. Penny Marshall, dir. *A League of Their Own* [Film] (Culver City, CA: Columbia Pictures, 1992).

7. Michael Vlessides, "Excessive Masculinity Linked to High Suicide Risk," *Medscape*, February 19, 2020, https://www.medscape.com/viewarticle/925447?nlid=134052_5402&src=wnl_dne_200220_mscpedit&uac=137938CZ&impID=2284655&faf=1.

8. Kristoffer Henriksen, Robert Schinke, Karin Moesch, Sean McCann, William D. Parham, Carsten Hvid Larsen, and Peter Terry, "Consensus Statement on Improving the Mental Health of High-Performance Athletes," *International Journal of Sport and Exercise Psychology* 18, no. 5 (2019): 1–8, https://doi.org/10.1080/1612197X.2019.1570473.

9. Kevin Love, "Everyone Is Going Through Something," *Players Tribune*, March 6, 2018, https://www.theplayerstribune.com/en-us/articles/kevin-love-everyone-is-going-through-something.

10. Headspace, "Mindfulness," https://www.headspace.com/mindfulness.

11. Richard H. Ackerman and Patrick Maslin-Ostrowski, *The Wounded Leader: How Real Leadership Emerges in Times of Crisis* (San Francisco: Jossey-Bass, 2002).

12. Daniel Gould and Jenny Nalepa, "Coaching Club and Scholastic Sports," in *Coach Education Essentials: Your Guide to Developing Sport Coaches*, edited by Kristen Dieffenbach and Melissa Thompson (Champaign, IL: Human Kinetics, 2020), 111–30.

13. Amanda J. Visek, Sara M. Achrati, Heather M. Mannix, Karen McDonnell, Brandonn S. Harris, and Loretta DiPietro, "The Fun Integration Theory: Toward Sustaining Children and Adolescents Sport Participation," *Journal of Physical Activity & Health* 12, no. 3 (2015): 424–33, https://doi.org/10.1123/jpah.2013-0180.

14. Melissa Healy, "Suicide Rates for US Teens and Young Adults Are the Highest on Record," *Los Angeles Times*, June 18, 2019, https://www.latimes.com/science/la-sci-suicide-rates-rising-teens-young-adults-20190618-story.html.

15. University of Oklahoma, "Suicide Prevention Resource Center," https://www.sprc.org/.

16. Substance Abuse and Mental Health Services Administration, *Preventing Suicide: A Toolkit for High Schools* (Rockville, MD: U.S. Department of Health & Human Services, 2012).

17. Cecile Reynaud, "College and High-Level Amateur Sports," in *Coach Education Essentials: Your Guide to Developing Sport Coaches*, edited by Kristen Dieffenbach and Melissa Thompson (Champaign, IL: Human Kinetics, 2020), 131–54.

CHAPTER 4

1. David Epstein, *Range: Why Generalists Triumph in a Specialized World* (New York: Riverhead Books, 2019); John Kessel, "'Ancora Imparo'—Secrets Learned in 50 Years of Coaching around the World," keynote address at the United States Center for Coaching Excellence 2019 Summit, Colorado Springs, CO, June 18, 2019.

2. Andy Puddicombe and Ryan Flaherty, "Stronger Mind, Stronger Body," produced by Nike, *Trained* [podcast], August 9, 2018, https://podtail.com/en/podcast/trained/andy-puddicombe-strong-mind-stronger-body/.

3. Aspen Institute, Project Play, https://www.aspenprojectplay.org/.

4. Jessica Lahey, *The Gift of Failure: How the Best Parents Learn to Let Go So Their Children Can Succeed* (New York: Harper Collins, 2015).

5. Carol Dweck, *Mindsets* (New York: Ballantine Books, 2006).

6. Mark Bisson, *Coach Yourself First: A Coach's Guide to Self-Reflection* (Market Harborough, UK: Troubadour, 2017).

7. L. S. Vygotsky, *Mind in Society: The Development of Higher Psychological Processes*, edited by Michael Cole, Vera John-Steiner, Sylvia Scribner, and Ellen Souberma (Cambridge, MA: Harvard University Press, 1978).

8. Mihaly Csikszentmihalyi, *Flow: The Psychology of Optimal Experience* (New York: Harper & Row, 1990).

9. Simon Sinek, "Find fulfillment—Find Your WHY," YouTube, December 9, 2015, https://www.youtube.com/watch?v=rvqvLF5UpRk.

10. Sarah McQuade, "How to Learn as a Coach from Self-Reflection," *USA Football Blogs* [blog], December 29, 2017, https://blogs.usafootball.com/blog/5257/how-to-learn-as-a-coach-from-self-reflection.

11. Pat Summitt, *Reach for the Summit: The Definite Dozen System for Succeeding at Whatever You Do* (New York: Three Rivers Press, 1999).

CHAPTER 5

1. Dev Roychowdhury, "Spiritual Well-Being in Sport and Exercise Psychology," *SAGE Open* 9, no. 1 (March 13, 2019): 1–6, https://journals.sagepub.com/doi/full/10.1177/2158244019837460.

2. Peter M. Senge, *The Fifth Discipline: The Art and Practice of the Learning Organization*, 2nd ed. (New York: Doubleday, 2006).

3. Melissa Thompson, "Ethical and Philosophical Grounding of Coaches," in *Coach Education Essentials: Your Guide to Developing Sport Coaches*, edited by Kristen Dieffenbach and Melissa Thompson (Champaign, IL: Human Kinetics, 2020), 17–34.

4. Daniel H. Pink, *Drive: The Surprising Truth about What Motivates Us* (New York: Penguin Random House, 2009).

CHAPTER 6

1. Brad Nein, "Creating a Positive Sports Environment," *Educated Coaches*, April 7, 2015, https://educatedcoaches.com/2015/04/07/create-a-positive-sports-environment/.

2. Jim Taylor, "Build a Team Culture for Athletic Success," *Psychology Today*, September 17, 2016, https://www.psychologytoday.com/us/blog/the-power-prime/201609/build-team-culture-athletic-success.

3. Antonia Rudenstine, Sydney Schaef, and Dixie Bacallao, "Meeting Students Where They Are," National Summit on K-12 Competency-Based Education for the International Association for K–12 Online Learning (2017), https://www.inacol.org/wp-content/uploads/2017/06/CompetencyWorks-MeetingStudentsWhereTheyAre2.pdf.

4. Isaac Prilleltensky, "Wellness as Fairness," *American Journal of Community Psychology* 49, no. 1–2 (2012): 1–21, http://doi.org/10.1007/s10464-011-9448-8; Stephanie M. Reich, Manuel Riemer, Isaac Prilleltensky, and Maritza Montero, eds. *International Community Psychology: History and Theories* (Irvine, CA: Springer, 2007).

5. James Sudakow, "If You Don't Build Your Culture, One Will Form on Its Own (and You Might Not Like What You Get): Why Your Culture Is at Risk If You Don't Build It with the Same Level of Investment You Would Make for Any Other Strategic Company Initiative," *Inc.*, February 23, 2017, https://www.inc.com/james-

sudakow/if-you-dont-build-your-culture-one-will-form-on-its-own-and-you-might-not-like-w.html; Taylor, "Build a Team Culture for Athletic Success."

6. Frank J. Barrett and Ronald E. Fry, *Appreciative Inquiry: A Positive Approach to Building Cooperative Capacity* (Chagrin Falls, OH: Taos Institute Publications, 2008).

7. Carol Dweck, *Mindsets* (New York: Ballantine Books, 2006).

8. Cara Cocchiarella, *The Effect of Community Service Participation on Team Cohesiveness in NCAA Division I Women's Volleyball Teams* (EdD diss., University of Montana, 2015).

CHAPTER 7

1. American Public Health Association, "Health Equity," https://www.apha.org/Topics-and-Issues/Health-Equity.

2. Matthew Stevens, "Sports Are a Microcosm of Today's Broken Society," *Fan Nation*, June 1, 2020, https://www.si.com/college/illinois/olympic-sports/illini-now-matthew-stevens-column-society-and-sports-june-1-2020.

3. George B. Cunningham, "The Under-Representation of Racial Minorities in Coaching and Leadership Positions in the United States," in *"Race," Ethnicity and Racism in Sports Coaching*, edited by Steven Bradbury, Jim Lusted, and Jacco van Sterkenburg (London and New York: Routledge, 2020), 3–21.

4. Harry Edwards, "Crisis of Black Athletes on the Eve of the 21st Century," *Society* 37 (2000): 9–13, https://doi.org/10.1007/BF02686167.

5. Stevens, "Sports Are a Microcosm of Today's Broken Society"; Cunningham, "The Under-Representation of Racial Minorities in Coaching and Leadership Positions in the United States."

6. Kristen Dieffenbach and John O'Sullivan, "#102: Is There a Difference between Coaching Girls and Coaching Boys?" produced by Changing the Game Project, *Way of Champions Podcast*, February 17, 2019, https://changingthegameproject.com/is-there-a-difference-between-coaching-girls-and-coaching-boys-with-dr-kristen-dieffenbach/.

7. Dieffenback and O'Sullivan, "#102: Is There a Difference between Coaching Girls and Coaching Boys?"

8. WeCOACH, https://wecoachsports.org/.

9. Nicole M. LaVoi, Courtney Boucher, and Sarah Silbert, *Head Coaches of Women's Collegiate Teams: A Comprehensive Report on NCAA Division-I Institutions, 2018–19* (Minneapolis, MN: University of Minnesota, The Tucker Center for Research on Girls & Women in Sport, 2019); NCAA, NCAA Demographics Database, 2020, https://www.ncaa.org/about/resources/research/ncaa-demographics-database.

10. National Coalition of Anti-Violence Programs, *Lesbian, Gay, Bisexual, Transgender, Queer, and HIV-Affected Hate and Intimate Partner Violence in 2017* (New York: New York City Gay and Lesbian Anti-Violence Project, 2018), http://avp.org/wp-content/uploads/2019/01/NCAVP-HV-IPV-2017-report.pdf.

CHAPTER 8

1. NCAA, *NCAA Recruiting Facts* (2018), https://collegiatewaterpolo.org/wp-content/uploads/2020/07/NCAARecruiting-Fact-Sheet-WEB.pdf.

2. Cathy Ericson, "What Financial Athletes Can Teach You about Money," *Forbes*, January 6, 2015, https://www.forbes.com/sites/learnvest/2015/01/06/what-financial-athletes-can-teach-you-about-managing-your-money/#63b1fa27749c.

3. Michael Casey, "Want to Succeed in Business? Then Play High School Sports," *Fortune*, June 19, 2014, https://fortune.com/2014/06/19/high-school-sports-business-cornell-job-market/.

4. Brett Rapkin, dir., *The Weight of Gold* (New York: HBO, 2020), https://www.hbo.com/documentaries/the-weight-of-gold.

5. Pablo S. Torre, "How (and Why) Athletes Go Broke," *Sports Illustrated Vault*, March 23, 2009, https://www.si.com/vault/2009/03/23/105789480/how-and-why-athletes-go-broke; Emma Vickers, "Life after Sport: Depression in the Retired Athlete," *Believe Perform*, https://believeperform.com/life-after-sport-depression-in-retired-athletes/.

6. Corliss Bean, Sara Kramers, Tanya Forneris, and Martin Camiré, "The Implicit/Explicit Continuum of Life Skills Development and Transfer," *Quest* 70, no. 4 (2018): 456–70, https://doi.org/10.1080/00336297.2018.1451348.

7. Christian Jarrett, "Learning by Teaching Others is Extremely Effective—A New Study Tested the Key to Why," *British Psychological Society*, May 4, 2018. https://digest.bps.org.uk/2018/05/04/learning-by-teaching-others-is-extremely-effective-a-new-study-tested-a-key-reason-why/; Logan Fiorella and Richard E. Mayer, "The

Relative Benefits of Learning by Teaching and Teaching Expectancy," *Contemporary Educational Psychology* 38, no. 4 (2013): 281–88, https://doi.org/10.1016/j .cedpsych.2013.06.001.

CHAPTER 9

1. Aspen Institute, Project Play, https://www.aspenprojectplay.org/.

2. Aspen Institute, *State of Play Seattle—King County: Analysis and Recommendations* (2019), http://uwcla.uw.edu/sites/default/files/2019-09/2019%20 SOP%20Seattle-KingCounty%20Web%20FINAL.pdf.

3. Dave Egner, "Wilson Foundation CEO: 'This Is about Civilization and Developing Leaders Moving Forward,'" interview by the Aspen Institute, February 28, 2019, https://www.aspenprojectplay.org/project-play-2024/spotlight/dave-egner-rcwjrf.

4. Wade Gilbert, *Coaching Better Every Season: A Year-Round System for Athlete Development and Program Success* (Champaign, IL: Human Kinetics, 2017).

5. Baseball Beyond Borders, "Moving Beyond 12," https://baseballbeyond.org/mb12.

Selected Bibliography

The following resources provide substantial contributions to the foundation for wellness in coaching and coach development. This list is intended to enhance readers' exploration of research and best practices in the field of coaching as wellness and coach development continue to advance. Where possible, a general website or collection of sources is provided as opposed to a singular work.

Aspen Institute. Project Play. https://www.aspenprojectplay.org/.

Balyi, Istvan, Richard Way, and Colin Higgs. *Long-Term Athlete Development*. Champaign, IL: Human Kinetics, 2013.

Brady, Abbe, and Bridget Grenville-Cleave. *Positive Psychology in Sport and Physical Activity: An Introduction*. New York: Routledge, 2018.

Brown, Brené. https://brenebrown.com/.

Callery, Bettina, and Brian Gearity, eds. *Coach Education and Development in Sport: Instructional Strategies*. New York: Routledge, 2020.

Changing the Game Project. "Changing the Game Project: Parents and Coaches." 2020. https://changingthegameproject.com/parent-coaches/.

Côté, Jean, and Wade Gilbert. "An Integrative Definition of Coaching Effectiveness and Expertise." *International Journal of Sports Science and Coaching* 4 (2009): 307–23. https://doi.org/10.1260/174795409789623892.

Dieffenbach, Kristen, and Melissa Thompson, eds. *Coach Education Essentials: Your Guide to Developing Sport Coaches*. Champaign, IL: Human Kinetics, 2020.

Dweck, Carol. *Mindsets*. New York: Ballantine, 2006.

Gano-Overway, Lori, Melissa Thompson, and Pete Van Mullem. *National Standards for Sport Coaches: Quality Coaches, Quality Sports*. Burlington, MA: Jones & Bartlett Learning, 2021.

International Council for Coaching Excellence and Association of Summer Olympic International Federations. *International Sport Coaching Framework: Version 1.1*. 2012. https://www.icce.ws/_assets/files/news/ISCF_1_aug_2012.pdf.

Mann, Amanendra, and Bani Narula. "Positive Psychology in Sports: An Overview." *International Journal of Social Science* 6, no. 2 (2017): 153–58. https://doi .org/10.5958/2321–5771.2017.00017.5.

National Council of Youth Sports. "Education: How to Coach Kids." 2020. https:// www.ncys.org/education/how-to-coach-kids/.

NCAA Sport Science Institute. "Nutrition, Sleep, and Performance Educational Resources." 2019. http://www.ncaa.org/sport-science-institute/nutrition-sleep-and-performance-educational-resources.

Positive Coaching Alliance. https://positivecoach.org/.

Ryan, Richard M., and Edward L. Deci. "Self-Determination Theory and the Facilitation of Intrinsic Motivation, Social Development, and Well-Being." *American Psychologist* 55, no. 1 (2000): 68–78. https://selfdeterminationtheory .org/SDT/documents/2000_RyanDeci_SDT.pdf.

Seligman, Martin E. P., and Mihaly Csikszentmihaly. "Positive Psychology: An Introduction." *American Psychologist* 55 (2000): 5–14. https://doi .org/10.1037/0003–066X.55.1.5.

SHAPE (Society of Health and Physical Educators) America. "National Standards for Sport Coaches." 2021. https://www.shapeamerica.org/standards/coaching/ default.aspx.

Siwik, Mark, Alan Lambert, Doug Saylor, Rachael Bertram, Cara Cocchiarella, and Wade Gilbert. "Long Term Program Development (LTPD): An Interdisciplinary Framework for Developing Athletes, Coaches, and Sport Programs." *International Sport Coaching Journal* 2, no. 3 (2015): 305–16. https://doi.org/10.1123/iscj.2015–0075.

Substance Abuse and Mental Health Services Administration. *Creating a Healthier Life: A Step-by-Step Guide to Wellness*. 2016. https://store.samhsa.gov/sites/default/files/d7/priv/sma16–4958.pdf.

Turnbridge, Jennifer, and Jean Côté. "Applying Transformational Leadership Theory to Coaching Research in Youth Sport: A Systematic Literature Review." *International Journal of Sport and Exercise Psychology* 16, no. 3 (2018): 327–42. https://doi.org/10.1080/1612197X.2016.1189948.

United States Center for Coaching Excellence. https://www.qualitycoachingeducation.org/.

United States Olympic and Paralympic Committee. "Quality Coaching Framework." 2020. https://www.teamusa.org/About-the-USOPC/Programs/Coaching-Education/Quality-Coaching-Framework.

University of Washington, Center for Leadership in Athletics. http://uwcla.uw.edu/.

Index

Page references for figures are italicized.

About the Authors

Cara Cocchiarella, EdD, is a coach developer with Win Win Consulting and a professor in health and physical education. She has proven success coaching athletes from kindergarten through college in seven different sports, earning numerous trophies and coach of the year honors. Dr. Cocchiarella is dedicated to empowering sports leaders in pursuit of excellence and ensuring access and quality programming for all athletes. Her continued service to the field of coach development is driven by her passion for inclusive, holistic, athlete-centered coaching and the potential for sports to enrich all of our lives. For more information or to contact Dr. Cocchiarella, go to https://www.winwin-consulting.com/.

Camille Adana is a health educator, coach, and author of *Motivate from Within: A Young Adult's Guide to Shooting for the Stars*, and founder of Adana Dynamics. She has inspired a variety of different athletes at the high school level in volleyball, basketball, softball, and cross country. Adana's coaching style promotes determination, grit, accountability, and empathy in athletics and everyday life. Community is at the heart of her work, with the goal to impact the village raising our children today. Adana strives for heartfelt human connection through conversations to ignite passion and guide people to live the best version of themselves while ultimately striving to feel well in all aspects of their lives. For more information or to contact Adana, go to http://www.adanadynamics.com/.

Lightning Source UK Ltd.
Milton Keynes UK
UKHW041257010722
405244UK00009B/132